LONGMAN

KEYSTONE

Phonics and Word Analysis

PEARSON
Longman

Longman Keystone
Phonics and Word Analysis

Pearson Education, 10 Bank Street, White Plains, NY 10606

Staff credits: The people who made up the *Longman Keystone* team, representing editorial, production, design, manufacturing, and marketing, are John Ade, Rhea Banker, Liz Barker, Danielle Belfiore, Don Bensey, Virginia Bernard, Kenna Bourke, Brandon Carda, Mindy DePalma, Johnnie Farmer, Maryann Finocchi, Patrice Fraccio, Geraldine Geniusas, Charles Green, Zach Halper, Henry Hild, David L. Jones, Ed Lamprich, Jamie Lawrence, Emily Lippincott, Maria Pia Marrella, Linda Moser, Laurie Neaman, Sherri Pemberton, Lisa Pleva, Joan Poole, Edie Pullman, Monica Rodriguez, Tara Rose, Tania Saiz-Sousa, Donna Schaffer, Chris Siley, Lynn Sobotta, Heather St. Clair, Jennifer Stem, Siobhan Sullivan, Jane Townsend, Heather Vomero, Marian Wassner, Lauren Weidenman, Matthew Williams, and Adina Zoltan.

Text design and composition: TSI Graphics
Photo credits: shutterstock.com

ISBN-13: 978-0-13-713830-2
ISBN-10: 0-13-713830-X

PEARSON LONGMAN ON THE **WEB**

Pearsonlongman.com offers online resources for teachers and students. Access our Companion Websites, our online catalog, and our local offices around the world.

Visit us at **www.pearsonlongman.com.**

Printed in the United States of America
7 8 9 10—V011—12 11

Contents

Alphabet Review 1
Consonant Sound-Spelling Review 3
Chapter 1: Short Vowels 7
Chapter 2: Consonant Blends 29
Chapter 3: Long Vowels. 47
Chapter 4: Contractions and Consonant Digraphs 85
Chapter 5: R-controlled Vowels 107
Chapter 6: Vowel Teams 127
Chapter 7: Silent Letters 153
Chapter 8: Word Analysis 171
Consonant Reminders. 185
Vowel Reminders 186
Vowel and Syllable Generalizations 187

ALPHABET REVIEW

A. Read the letters of the alphabet out loud. Notice that each letter has an uppercase and a lowercase.

Aa	Bb	Cc	Dd	Ee
Ff	Gg	Hh	Ii	Jj
Kk	Ll	Mm	Nn	Oo
Pp	Qq	Rr	Ss	Tt
Uu	Vv	Ww	Xx	Yy
Zz				

B. Write the uppercase and lowercase letters of the alphabet in your own chart below.

Alphabet Review

Remember that the alphabet has both consonants and vowels and that each letter has an uppercase and a lowercase.

A. Identify each consonant. Circle the corresponding lowercase letter.

1. C   a   y   c

2. P   p   j   k

3. T   m   o   t

4. R   r   l   x

5. Z   u   d   z

6. F   b   f   w

7. S   n   s   g

8. H   h   i   q

9. B   s   d   b

10. Q   r   q   g

11. D   d   b   f

B. Identify each vowel. Circle the corresponding uppercase letter.

1. o   D   Q   O

2. a   A   M   N

3. e   F   E   S

4. u   W   U   V

5. i   L   T   I

CONSONANT SOUND-SPELLING REVIEW

These letters are consonants: *b, c, d, f, g, h, j, k, l, m, n, p, q, r, s, t, v, w, x, y, z.*

Review the sounds these consonants stand for: *b, c, k, s, t.*

The letter *b* stands for the /b/ sound, as in *bed.*
The letter *c* can stand for the /k/ sound, as in *cat* or the /s/ sound, as in *city.*
The letter *k* stands for the /k/ sound, as in *kid.*
The letters *ck* together also stand for the /k/ sound, as in *back.* Notice that the *c* is silent.
The letter *s* stands for the /s/ sound, as in *sad.*
The letter *t* stands for the /t/ sound, as in *tap.*

A. Look at each picture and say its name. Circle the letter that stands for the sound each picture begins with.

1.	d	(b)	c
2.	j	c	t
3.	k	n	s
4.	p	s	w
5.	t	h	j

B. In the space below, write words you know that have the /k/ sound.

Consonant Sound-Spelling Review

CONSONANT SOUND-SPELLING REVIEW

Review the sounds these consonants stand for: *g, j, l, p, r, v.*

The letter *g* can stand for the /g/ sound, as in *gap*, or the /j/ sound, as in *age*.
The letter *j* stands for the /j/ sound, as in *jet*.
The letter *l* stands for the /l/ sound, as in *lid*.
The letter *p* stands for the /p/ sound, as in *pick*.
The letter *r* stands for the /r/ sound, as in *rap*.
The letter *v* stands for the /v/ sound, as in *vet*.

A. Look at each picture and say its name. Draw a line to match each picture name to the letter that stands for the sound it begins with.

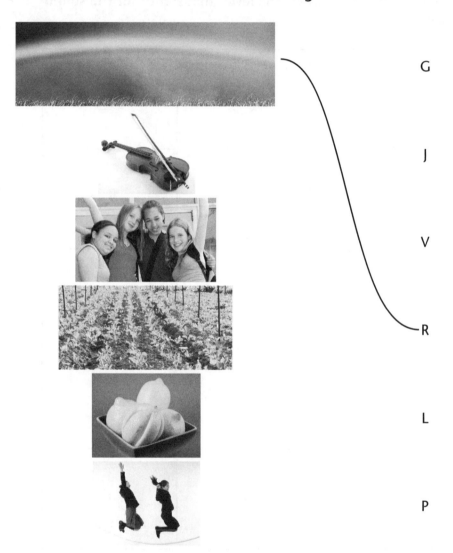

G

J

V

R

L

P

B. On the line below, write words you know that have the /j/ sound.

_____

Consonant Sound-Spelling Review

CONSONANT SOUND-SPELLING REVIEW

Review the sounds these letters stand for: *m, d, qu, y, n.*

The letter *m* stands for the /m/ sound, as in *mud.*
The letter *d* stands for the /d/ sound, as in *dip.*
The letters *qu* stand for the /kw/ sound, as in *quit.*
The letter *y* stands for the /y/ sound, as in *yes.*
The letter *n* stands for the /n/ sound, as in *nod.*

A. Look at each picture and say its name. Circle the letter or letters that stand for the sound each picture name begins with.

1.	n	t	m
2.	d	f	g
3.	qu	kw	w
4.	s	m	y
5.	d	v	n

B. On the line below, write words you know that have the /d/ sound.

_____

CONSONANT SOUND-SPELLING REVIEW

Review the sounds these consonants stand for: *f, h, w, x, z.*

The letter *f* stands for the /f/ sound, as in *fit.*
The letter *h* stands for the /h/ sound, as in *hid.*
The letter *w* stands for the /w/ sound, as in *wet.*
The letter *x* can stand for the /ks/ sound, as in *fox,* or the /z/ sound, as in *Xavier.*
The letter *z* stands for the /z/ sound, as in *zip.*

A. Look at each picture and say its name. Write the letter that stands for the sound that each picture name begins with.

 1.  _____

3.  _____

2.  _____

4.  _____

B. Look at each picture and say its name. Write the letter or letters that stand for the final sound that each picture name ends with.

1.  _____

3.  _____

2.  _____

4.  _____

Consonant Sound-Spelling Review

CHAPTER 1   **SHORT VOWELS**

Short *a*..8

High Frequency Words: Set 1 10

Reading Practice: Passage 1 11

Short *i*... 12

Short *o*... 14

Consonant *s*: /z/ Sound......................... 16

Word Analysis: Inflection: *-s*................... 17

Final Double Consonants 18

Short *e* 19

High Frequency Words: Set 2 21

Reading Practice: Passage 2..................... 22

Short *u*.. 23

Word Analysis: Possessives with *'s*.............. 25

Word Analysis:
    CVC Syllables and Phonograms 26

Chapter 1 Review................................. 28

SHORT *a*

The letter a can stand for the short vowel sound /a/, as in *at*. The /a/ sound sometimes comes at the beginning of words.

A. Look at the pictures. Write the letters to complete the words. Then read the words out loud.

— — ple   — — t   — — — — gator

B. Read the following words out loud. Circle the words that have the short vowel sound /a/.

1. can   (bad)   bin

2. am   in   ad

3. an   dad   sit

4. dip   dab   at

5. had   hat   hot

C. Complete each sentence with a word from the box below. Then read the sentences out loud.

| act   ad   after   answer |

1. Sam will _____ in the play.

2. I don't know the _____ to that question.

3. Let's meet _____ school.

4. I saw an _____ for the computer I want.

SHORT *a*

The letter *a* can stand for the short vowel sound /a/, as in *cat*. The /a/ sound sometimes comes in the middle of words.

A. Look at the pictures. Write the letters to complete the words. Then read the words out loud.

— — —   — — —   — — —

B. Read the following sentences out loud. Circle the words that have the short vowel sound /a/.

1. I had a fat cat.

2. A cat had a nap.

3. I had a hat.

4. Dan ran fast.

5. I am glad to see Dad.

6. Sam had a rat.

C. Complete each sentence with a word from the box below.

cap   cat   fat   had   tan

1. The name of my _____*cat*_____ is Mittens.

2. The _____ keeps his head warm.

3. I _____ three eggs this morning.

4. Pam had a _____ from the sun.

5. Hal had a _____ cat.

A. **You will see these ten words in many books. Read the words out loud.**

are is like me see that the to what you

B. **Read the following sentences out loud. Then circle the high frequency words.**

1. What is that?

2. That is a cat.

3. I like that cat.

4. What is the cat like?

5. That cat is fat.

6. The cat can see a rat.

7. The rat is sad to see the cat.

8. The rat ran to that bag.

9. Are you Pam?

10. That is me.

11. Is that Sam?

12. It is.

C. **Read the sentences again. Answer the following questions.**

1. What is the cat like?

   _____

2. Who is sad to see the cat?

   _____

READING PRACTICE: Passage 1

A. Read the following passage out loud.

Hal and Sam

A man had a cat.
A man had a black cat.

Is that man Hal?
That man is Hal.
Hal has a cat.
Hal has a black cat.

Is that black cat Sam?
That black cat is Sam.
Sam is Hal's black cat.

Hal can pat Sam.
Sam can purr for Hal.
Hal and Sam can nap.

Sam can tag Hal.
Hal can tag Sam.
Hal and Sam can play tag.

Sam is a pal to Hal.
Hal is a pal to Sam.
Sam and Hal are happy.

B. Read the passage again. Answer the following questions.

What is the man's name? What does the man have?

_____

 Read the passage to a family member or a friend. Ask him or her to read it again with you.

SHORT *i*

The letter *i* can stand for the short vowel sound /i/, as in *it*. The /i/ sound sometimes comes at the beginning of words.

A. Look at the pictures. Write the letters to complete the words. Then read the words out loud.

__ __ loo

__ gu __ __ __

__ __ __ ect

B. Complete the following words with the short vowel /i/. Then read the words out loud.

1. _*i*_nside

2. ___llness

3. ___nvent

4. ___nteresting

C. Complete each sentence with a word from the box below. You will use each word more than once. Then read the sentences out loud.

| if | in | is | it |

1. Tom _____*is*_____ a pal to Dan.

2. A map is _____ the van.

3. What _____ in this soup?

4. What _____ Tim is mad?

5. Sal is _____ the cab.

6. Is _____ okay to pet the cat?

SHORT *i*

The letter *i* can stand for the short vowel sound /i/, as in *him*. The /i/ sound often comes in the middle of words.

A. Look at the pictures. Write the letters to complete the words. Then read the words out loud.

_ _ g

_ _ p

B. Read the following sentences out loud. Circle the words that have the short vowel sound /i/.

1. (Did) the cat (nip) at (Tim)?

2. I hid the tin can.

3. Jim can sit in the rig.

4. The pig had a fig.

5. The cat bit the big rat.

C. Read the following words out loud. Find and circle the words.

am   an   at   big   can   cat   did   had   if   in   is   it   jam   pig   ran   six

b	i	g	i	t	a	t	i	s	w	f
c	a	t	j	a	m	h	a	d	a	n
c	a	n	r	a	n	i	n	d	i	d
p	i	g	i	f	a	m	s	i	x	a

SHORT *o*

The letter *o* can stand for the short vowel sound /o/, as in *object*.

A. Look at the pictures. Write the letters to complete the words. Then read the words out loud.

__ live

__ ctag __ n

__ pera

B. Read the following sentences out loud. Circle the words that begin with the short vowel sound /o/.

1. I saw *Othello* at the opera last night.

2. The octopus is an odd animal.

3. In October, he obtained funding for his research.

4. The object of the game is to hit the orange ball.

5. It's obvious that he likes olives.

C. Circle the correct word to complete each sentence. Then read the sentences out loud.

1. What is on the (pot, top) of the hat?

2. Did Jim (jog, bog) to the rock?

3. The dog is (hot, hop).

4. The hog is on the (lop, rock).

5. I can (lock, lot) the box.

SHORT o

The letter *o* can stand for the short vowel sound /o/, as in *box*. The /o/ sound often comes in the middle of words.

A. Look at the pictures. Write the letters to complete the words. Then read the words out loud.

m __ p

f __ x

l __ ck

B. Complete each sentence with a word from the box below. Then read the sentences out loud.

| fox   hop   mop   pot   rot |

1. The _____ ran after the hen.

2. There is hot soup in the _____.

3. Please _____ the kitchen floor.

4. The rabbit can _____ in the grass.

5. A log will _____ in the woods.

C. Read the following sentences out loud. Then complete the chart with words that have the short vowel sounds /a/, /i/, and /o/.

It is hot.　　　　　　　Jim got a job at the dam.
The cat ran.　　　　　　Zack is not a bad dog.
The fox hid in the pit.　　Rick can pick the top hog.

/a/	/i/	/o/

Short Vowels • Chapter 1

CONSONANT *s*: /z/ Sound

The letter *s* can stand for the /z/ sound, as in *was*.

A. Complete each sentence with a word from the box below. You will use some words more than once.

as has his is whose

1. Sam _____*has*_____ a big dog.

2. _____ dog cannot sit on his lap.

3. _____ dog is that?

4. What _____ that dog like?

5. That dog is as good _____ gold.

6. It _____ not a bad dog.

B. Read the following sentences out loud. Circle the words that have the /z/ sound.

1. Those shoes have to be his.

2. Whose vase of roses is that?

3. This cheese soup is so easy to cook.

4. That bird makes a lot of noise.

5. The boys chose to drive their cars.

C. Read the following words out loud. Find and circle the words. You will find some words more than once.

is

as

his

has

w	z	a	i	h
h	h	a	s	h
a	i	s	z	w
s	s	s	i	s
i	h	a	s	s

WORD ANALYSIS: Inflection: -s

When s is added to a singular noun, the noun becomes plural. When s is added to a verb, the verb becomes the present tense when used with *he*, *she*, or *it*.

Nouns with -s	Verbs with -s
hats	sits
caps	picks
cans	likes

A. Complete each sentence by adding the correct form of the noun or verb in parentheses. Then read the sentences out loud.

1. Pam _____*likes*_____ (like) the hat.

2. Tom has six _____ (cat).

3. Did you see the trash _____ (bin)?

4. Tad _____ (dig) a hole in the sand.

5. Pick up the _____ (rag).

B. Read the following words out loud. First, circle the words with the inflection -s. Then add the inflection -s to the other words and write them on the lines.

1. cats   cot   _____*cots*_____

2. pat   pots   _____

3. sits   bat   _____

4. pick   packs   _____

5. hops   hip   _____

6. top   tips   _____

7. hats   ham   _____

8. socks   sack   _____

FINAL DOUBLE CONSONANTS

Sometimes a word will end with two consonants that are the same, as in *will*. We call these two letters a double consonant. A double consonant stands for one sound.

A. Read the following words out loud. Write the words that have the same final double consonants.

1. miss   hiss   will   _____   _____

2. hill   wish   bill   _____   _____

3. off   loft   tiff   _____   _____

4. bass   ball   mill   _____   _____

5. doll   fill   toss   _____   _____

6. pill   pass   moss   _____   _____

B. Read the following sentences out loud. Circle the words that have a final double consonant.

1. Dad will fill up the bag.

2. I will miss you.

3. The tops are off the cans.

4. The lid is off the pot.

5. The log has moss on it.

6. Did Mom kiss you?

7. Bill looks very ill.

8. The inn is full of people.

9. That snake will hiss and bite.

10. Did the bell toll this morning?

11. Do not yell at Nell.

Name _____ Date _____

SHORT e

The letter *e* can stand for the short vowel sound /e/, as in *elephants*. The /e/ sound sometimes comes at the beginning of words.

A. Look at the pictures. Write the letters to complete the words. Then read the words out loud.

__ __ g   __ __ pty   __ __ gine

B. Read the following sentences out loud. Then underline the words that have the short vowel sound /e/.

1. The <u>red</u> <u>hen</u> has <u>ten</u> <u>eggs</u>.

2. Jen tells him to sit on the bench.

3. Yes, I let the cat in the shed.

4. That jet will get you there.

5. Tell Ben to rest and to get well.

6. He fell and hurt his leg.

C. Complete each riddle with a word from the box below. Then read the riddles and the answers out loud.

bed   hen   pen   well

I peck in a pan.
I sit on eggs.
What am I?

_____*hen*_____

The tip of me has a nib.
I can dot an "i."
What am I?

_____

I am wet.
You can dip a pot in me.
What am I?

_____

I am big.
You can nap on me.
What am I?

_____

SHORT *e*

The letter *e* can stand for the short vowel sound /e/, as in *red*. The /e/ sound sometimes comes in the middle of words.

A. Look at the pictures. Write the letters to complete the words. Then read the words out loud.

__ __ d

__ __ n

__ __ ll

B. Read the following words out loud. Then write three words that rhyme with each.

1. hen   *ten*   _____   _____

2. bed   _____   _____   _____

3. let   _____   _____   _____

4. dent   _____   _____   _____

5. best   _____   _____   _____

C. Write words using the short vowel sounds /a/, /i/, /o/, and /e/.

1. p__n, d__n, t__n, h__n

2. b__d, r__d, f__d, m__d

3. l__t, p__t, s__t, d__t

4. b__g, w__g, r__g, t__g

5. t__p, p__p, m__p, l__p

6. p__ck, s__ck, l__ck, n__ck

HIGH FREQUENCY WORDS: Set 2

A. You will see these ten words in many books. Read the words out loud.

and does for he look make of one she your

B. Read the following sentences out loud. Circle the high frequency words.

1. Is he Rick?

2. Is she Tess?

3. Yes, he is Rick, and she is Tess.

4. Rick and Tess are pals.

5. Look for Tess, and you will see Rick.

6. He does what she does.

7. Rick will make a hat if Tess makes one.

8. If Tess gets a job, Rick will get one.

9. Tess will pack one of your bags.

10. Rick will pack ten of your bags.

11. He will not make your boss mad.

12. He will make it as one of the top dogs.

C. Read the sentences again. Answer the following questions.

1. Who will pack one of your bags?

_____

2. Who will make it as one of the top dogs?

_____

A. Read the following passage out loud.

Jam, Ham, and Eggs

Ann and Jack and I get out of bed.

It is time for a meal.

Ann can get jam.

Jam is good. Mmmm.

Jack can make ham.

Ham is good. Mmmm.

What can I make?

I can make eggs.

I pick six eggs.

I get a bowl.

I crack six eggs in a bowl.

I mix the eggs well.

I get a pan hot on the stove.

I put six eggs in a pan.

I let the eggs sit in the pan.

I flip the eggs.

I let the eggs sit in the pan.

Look! The eggs are hot. Mmmm.

I can make eggs well.

Ann, Jack, and I will eat a meal.

B. Read the passage again. Answer the following questions.

What did Ann and Jack eat? How many eggs did the writer crack?

_____

 Read the passage to a family member or a friend. Ask that person to tell you his or her favorite breakfast meal. Does he or she like eggs?

Name _____ Date _____

SHORT *u*

The letter *u* can stand for the short vowel sound /u/, as in *ugly*. The /u/ sound sometimes comes at the beginning of words.

A. Look at the pictures. Write the letters to complete the words. Then read the words out loud.

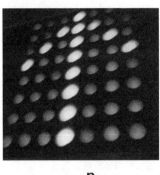

__ p   __ nd __ __ sh __ __ t   __ mb __ __ ll __

B. Read the following words out loud. Draw lines to connect the words that rhyme.

bun   tub

rub   fun

luck   rug

cup   tuck

dug   pup

C. Read the following sentences out loud. Circle the words that have the short vowel sound /u/.

1. I don't understand why he chose that university.

2. Unless we finish at the usual hour, we'll be unable to go.

3. He has an ugly scar under his knee.

4. The ultimate goal was to unite the groups.

5. His uniform was unacceptable.

The letter *u* can stand for the short vowel sound /u/, as in *tub*. The /u/ sound sometimes comes in the middle of words.

A. Look at the pictures. Write the letters to complete the words. Then read the words out loud.

— — — —

— — — — k

— — g

B. Read the following sentences out loud. Circle the words that have the short vowel sound /u/.

1. He fell in the ((mud), mug).

2. A grass (hut, tub) is on the hill.

3. The (mug, rug) is hot.

4. A (but, bug) is on that hat.

C. Read the following paragraph out loud. Then complete the chart with words that have the short vowel sounds /a/, /e/, /i/, /o/, and /u/.

Pup is a dog. He is a fun pet! He licks a lot. If he runs and digs in the mud, he has to get in the tub. I rub a rag on Pup.

/a/	/e/	/i/	/o/	/u/

Chapter 1 • Short Vowels

WORD ANALYSIS: Possessives with 's

Some nouns end with an apostrophe (') and the letter *s*. An *'s* shows ownership of something.

A. Read the examples in the box below.

Noun	Possessive
Pam	Pam's
Jim	Jim's
Pat	Pat's

B. Read the following sentences out loud. Underline the words that show ownership. Circle the words that tells what each person owns.

1. <u>Todd's</u> (hat) fell off.

2. Look for Jen's cot.

3. Ben's dog is big.

4. Bob's leg got cut.

5. Does Kim's pup like to run?

6. Tim's pen fell in the gap.

7. Is that Ken's map?

C. Read each name out loud. Add an *'s* to show ownership. Then write something that each one owns.

1. Tom   *Tom's car* _____

2. Tim   _____

3. cat   _____

4. dog   _____

5. Sam   _____

6. Bess _____

WORD ANALYSIS: CVC Syllables and Phonograms

Many words have the consonant-vowel-consonant, or CVC, pattern. This is also called a closed syllable. Notice that the vowel sound is closed in by two consonants.

Some CVC words share phonograms. A phonogram is a letter or set of letters that stand for a sound. You have already learned many phonograms, such as *b*, which stands for the /b/ sound, and *a*, which stands for the short /a/ sound.

Rhyming CVC words share the last two phonograms. We can group rhyming CVC words into word families.

A. Read the following words out loud. Then sort the words into word families and write the words in the correct columns.

bed cot fin fun jot led mat pin rat run red sat sun tin tot

-at	*-ot*	*-ed*	*-un*	*-in*

B. Read the following words out loud. Write a word that rhymes, or is in the same word family.

1. rip _____

2. mug _____

3. tap _____

4. sack _____

5. bet _____

CHAPTER 1 REVIEW

A. Complete each sentence by adding the inflection -s or a possessive 's. Then read the sentences out loud.

1. (Pam) _____ cat is on the bed.

2. I see the (pan) _____ but not the lids.

3. Look for (Jim) _____ hat.

4. He has (pin) _____ in that box.

5. (Mom) _____ leg got cut.

6. The sun (set) _____ at six o'clock.

7. Jan has the red (pen) _____.

8. (Todd) _____ mug is big.

9. Does Jess like (egg) _____?

10. Tell the (kid) _____ to run home.

B. Correct the underlined words by changing the vowel sounds. Then read the paragraph out loud.

Jen and Ken <u>set</u> on a rock. It was very <u>hat</u> outside.
    1.   2.

"Can you find the dam on that <u>mop</u>?"
                                3.

"I found it." Jen taps on the <u>mop</u>.
                                4.

Jen picks up Ken's back<u>pick</u>. Ken does <u>net</u> get up.
                        5.   6.

"Are you OK or are you <u>sack</u>?"
                        7.

"It's very sunny, and I am <u>hit</u>."
                            8.

"I can go to the dam and come <u>buck</u>. You can <u>nip</u>."
                                9.   10.

"OK. You can go see the dam. I <u>well</u> stay here and nap."
                                    11.

C. Read the following words out loud. Then write two words that rhyme with each.

1. pick   sick   _____   _____

2. bell   well   _____   _____

3. cut   but   _____   _____

4. tag   wag   _____   _____

5. pot   cot   _____   _____

6. lab   dab   _____   _____

7. tin   win   _____   _____

8. bun   sun   _____   _____

9. tap   zap   _____   _____

10. pill   hill   _____   _____

D. Read the following words out loud. Find and circle the words.

hams   his   hiss   off   well   wet   will   yes

w	y	a	h	i	s	s
w	e	i	h	i	s	f
i	s	t	w	e	l	l
l	s	l	o	f	f	s
l	y	h	a	m	s	s

CHAPTER 2   CONSONANT BLENDS

Initial Blends: *sp, st, sm*...... 30

Initial Blends: *sw, sn, sk, sl*...................... 31

Word Analysis: Inflections: *-ed, -ing* 32

High Frequency Words: Set 3 34

Reading Practice: Passage 3 35

Initial Blends: *tr, br, gr*........................... 36

Initial Blends: *fr, cr, pr* 37

Initial Blends: *cl, bl, gl* 38

Initial Blends: *fl, pl*............................. 39

High Frequency Words: Set 4 40

Reading Practice: Passage 4 41

Final Blends: *nt, nd* 42

Final Blends: *sp, st, lt, ld* 43

Final Digraph: *ng*; Final Blend: *nk*.............. 44

Chapter 2 Review 45

Name _____ Date _____

INITIAL BLENDS: *sp, st, sm*

In a consonant blend, two or three consonants appear together. Each consonant sound is pronounced. The blend sometimes comes at the beginning of a word.

- The blend *sp* sounds like /s//p/, as in *spill.*
- The blend *st* sounds like /s//t/, as in *stop.*
- The blend *sm* sounds like /s//m/, as in *smell.*

A. Look at the pictures. Read the following words out loud. Circle the initial blends.

spill

stop

smell

B. Read the following words out loud. Underline the words that begin with *sp*. Circle the words that begin with *st*. Box the words that begin with *sm*.

1. (stick)   <u>spell</u> | smack | 3. spot   still   smug

2. spin   smog   stop   4. step   span   smell

C. Complete each sentence with a word from the box below. Then read the sentences out loud.

| smack   smell   spins   stick   stop   stuck |

1. Lin _____*stuck*_____ a pin on her hat.

2. That is the bus _____.

3. The dog has a _____ in its mouth.

4. The wheel _____ around quickly.

5. I can _____ the coffee.

6. If you _____ the bug, it will make a mess.

Name _____ Date _____

INITIAL BLENDS: *sw, sn, sk, sl*

In a consonant blend, two or three consonants appear together. Each consonant sound is pronounced. The blend sometimes comes at the beginning of a word.

- The blend *sw* sounds like /s//w/, as in *swim*.
- The blend *sn* sounds like /s//n/, as in *snack*.
- The blend *sk* sounds like /s//k/, as in *skate*.
- The blend *sl* sounds like /s//l/, as in *sled*.

A. Look at the pictures. Read the following words out loud. Circle the initial blends.

swim

snack

skate

sled

B. Read the words out loud. Write a rhyming word that begins with *sw, sn, sk,* or *sl.*

1. bed _____   4. kid _____

2. tap _____   5. pack _____

3. lip _____   6. him _____

C. Complete each sentence with a word from the box below. Then read the sentences out loud.

| skin   sleeps   slip   snack   swim |

1. Did he _____*slip*_____ on the wet floor?

2. He sometimes _____ late.

3. The sun makes his _____ red.

4. He likes to jog, and she likes to _____.

5. I'm hungry for a _____.

WORD ANALYSIS: Inflections: -ed, -ing

The inflections -ed and -ing are added to the end of a base word to make a new word. Adding -ed changes a verb into the simple past. Adding -ing to a verb shows that the action continues over time. The -ing form is used with the verb be. Many base words do not change their spelling when you add -ed or -ing.

A. Read the following words out loud. Circle the inflections.

Base Word	-ing	-ed
pick	picking	picked
look	looking	looked
smell	smelling	smelled

B. Add the inflection -ed to each base word to change it into the simple past. Then read the words out loud.

1. fix _____*fixed*_____

2. pack _____

3. stack _____

4. lock _____

5. miss _____

6. spill _____

C. Complete each sentence by adding the inflection -ing to the word in parentheses. Then read the sentences out loud.

1. Pam is _____*picking*_____ (pick) up the cans.

2. You are_____ (go) to miss the bus!

3. Tom's dog is _____ (lick) his leg.

4. Dad is _____ (work) this weekend.

5. She is _____ (pack) a bag.

WORD ANALYSIS: Inflections: *-ed, -ing*

The spelling of a base word sometimes changes when *-ed* or *-ing* are added. When a base word has a short vowel sound and ends in a single consonant, the final consonant is doubled before adding *-ed* or *-ing*.

A. Read the following words out loud. Circle the inflections.

Base Word	*-ed*	*-ing*
jog	jogged	jogging
skip	skipped	skipping
bat	batted	batting

B. Fill in the line with either the *-ed* or *-ing* form of the base word. Then read the words out loud.

1. pat   patted   _____*patting*_____

2. beg   _____   begging

3. tug   _____   tugging

4. stop   stopped   _____

5. nod   nodded   _____

6. snap   _____   snapping

C. Write the correct form of the base word in parentheses. Then read the sentences out loud.

1. Pat is _____*swatting*_____ (swat) the bugs.

2. Mom is _____ (hug) me.

3. Why are you _____ (dig) in the mud?

4. Tim is _____ (jog) up to the dock.

5. Todd is _____ (sit) on the log.

6. Liz is _____ (spin) the top.

A. You will see these ten words in many books. Read the words out loud.

come do down find here my said they we where

B. Read the following sentences out loud. Then circle the high frequency words.

1. Ed cannot find Tim.

2. "Where is Tim?" Ed said to Biff.

3. "Tim is not here," said Biff.

4. "Is Tim down on the deck?" Ed said to Dan.

5. Dan said, "You will not find Tim on the deck."

6. "Where is my pal, Tim?" said Ed to Kim and Bill.

7. "What does Tim look like?" they said to Ed.

8. "We will find Tim," they said.

9. "Do you see Tim yet?" said Ed.

10. "Can you find my pal?" said Ed.

11. They looked and looked for Tim.

12. "Come here! Here is Tim!" Kim and Bill said to Ed.

13. Tim said, "Ed, where did you look for me?"

14. Ed said, "I looked down on the deck."

C. Read the sentences again. Answer the following questions.

1. Where did they look for Tim?

_____

2. Who said "Tim is not here"?

_____

READING PRACTICE: Passage 3

A. Read the following passage out loud.

Stan and His Sled

Stan got a sled. He sledded down a big hill. The hill was slick and fast. Stan sped down that hill. The sled slipped and skipped and slammed into a big red bin. Stan went plop.

Stan plopped on the hard snow. He sat up and rubbed his left leg. Stan saw the big red bin.

Stan picked himself up and ran to the top of a hill. He got on his sled and sledded down a big hill. The hill was slick and fast. The sled skipped and slipped.

Stan did not hit the big red bin. Stan sledded past the bin. Stan sledded to the end of the hill.

Stan stopped and got off his sled. Stan ran back up the hill.

Stan got back on his sled. He sledded and sledded. Stan had a fun time.

B. Read the passage again. Answer the following questions.

1. What did Stan get?

   _____

2. What did Stan's sled slam into?

   _____

Home-School Connection Read the passage to a family member or a friend. Discuss how to be safe when sledding. Do you think Sam was careful?

INITIAL BLENDS: *tr, br, gr*

In a consonant blend, two or three consonants appear together. Each consonant sound is pronounced. The blend sometimes comes at the beginning of a word.

- The blend *tr* sounds like /t//r/, as in *track*.
- The blend *br* sounds like /b//r/, as in *brick*.
- The blend *gr* sounds like /g//r/, as in *grin*.

A. Look at the pictures. Read the following words out loud. Circle the initial blends.

track

brick

grin

B. Read the following words out loud. Find and circle the words.

brick	grab	grin	grip
trap	trim	trip	truck

a	g	r	i	n	b
t	t	r	a	p	r
r	p	t	a	e	i
u	i	r	r	b	c
c	r	i	h	i	k
k	g	m	k	l	p

C. Add *tr, br,* or *gr* to complete the word in each sentence. Write the word on the line. Then read the sentences out loud.

1. We can sit in the ___*tr*___uck.   ___*truck*___

2. Tell Tom to _____ab the keys.   _____

3. I will _____im your hair.   _____

4. Fill the cup up to the _____im.   _____

Name _____ Date _____

INITIAL BLENDS: *fr, cr, pr*

In a consonant blend, two or three consonants appear together. Each consonant sound is pronounced. The blend sometimes comes at the beginning of a word.

- The blend *fr* sounds like /f//r/, as in *frog*.
- The blend *cr* sounds like /c//r/, as in *crab*.
- The blend *pr* sounds like /p//r/, as in *prom*.

A. Look at the pictures. Read the following words out loud. Circle the initial blends.

frog

crab

presents

B. Read the words out loud. Circle the two words in each line that have the same initial blend. Then write your own word with the same initial blend.

1. fad (Fred) (frizz) _____*frog*_____

2. cross   cram   come   _____

3. prick   pin   prod   _____

C. Read the following sentences out loud. Write the words with *fr, cr,* and *pr*.

1. For Jan Prinn, press 'one'. _____*Prinn, press*_____

2. That egg is cracked. _____

3. Fran's tot is in the crib. _____

4. Your prom frock has a lot of frills. _____

5. Kiss a lot of frogs to get a prince. _____

6. Ann crossed the creek. _____

7. That crock pot is Fred's. _____

INITIAL BLENDS: *cl, bl, gl*

In a consonant blend, two or three consonants appear together. Each consonant sound is pronounced. The blend sometimes comes at the beginning of a word.

- The blend *cl* sounds like /c//l/, as in *clock*.
- The blend *bl* sounds like /b//l/, as in *block*.
- The blend *gl* sounds like /g//l/, as in *glass*.

A. Look at the pictures. Read the following words out loud. Circle the initial blends.

clock

block

glass

B. Complete each word by adding *cl, bl,* or *gl* to the letters below. Then read the words out loud.

1. ____*cl*____ap

4. _____ad

2. _____ack

5. _____ock

3. _____ip

6. _____ob

C. Complete each sentence with a word from the box below. Then read the sentences out loud.

| black   block   clap   class   clip   glad |

1. Dad had to _____*clip*_____ the grass.

2. Fred was _____ Stan was here.

3. Miss Kim said, "Our _____ starts at ten o'clock."

4. Get a _____ and put it on the stack.

5. Hip-hop music makes me snap and _____.

6. Does the _____ top fit you well?

Chapter 2 • Consonant Blends

Name _____ Date _____

INITIAL BLENDS: *fl, pl*

In a consonant blend, two or three consonants appear together. Each consonant sound is pronounced. The blend sometimes comes at the beginning of a word.

- The blend *fl* sounds like /f//l/, as in *flag*.
- The blend *pl* sounds like /p//l/, as in *plug*.

A. Look at the pictures. Read the following words out loud. Circle the initial blends.

flag

flip

plug

B. Read the words in the box below out loud. Underline the words with initial blend *fl*. Circle the words with initial blend *pl*.

fan	flap	flat	flip	flop	lad
lid	pat	plan	plop	plot	pop

C. Circle the correct word to complete each sentence. Write the word on the line. Then read the sentences out loud.

1. My (plan, flan) is to find a big box for the dolls. _____*plan*_____

2. The top of it is (plat, flat). _____

3. Push mud in the crack to (plug, flug) it up. _____

4. Ten (plus, flus) six is sixteen. _____

5. The U.S. (plag, flag) has red at the top. _____

6. A (plum, flum) makes a good snack. _____

HIGH FREQUENCY WORDS: Set 4

A. You will see these ten words in many books. Read the words out loud.

funny	go	have	little	now	ride	saw	school	this	want

B. Read the following passage out loud. Then circle the high frequency words.

I ride the school bus to school. I have fun looking at stuff as we go. I saw a funny dog run down a hill on his little legs.

"Come here," I said to Val. "Look at the funny little dog run."

We saw a truck with logs stacked up on the back. We saw a cat flopped down in the grass. Now I do not want this ride to stop. I see the school. Now I will have to get down off of this bus. I am glad I get to ride the school bus to school.

C. Read the passage again. Answer the following questions.

1. Where does the bus go?

____

2. What did the writer see along the way?

____

Name _____ Date _____

A. **Read the following passage out loud.**

Get a Job!

Get out of bed. Put on tan pants and a black top. Get a JOB!

Moms and dads beg and yell at kids to get a job.

If you like cats and dogs, you can pet sit. Put milk in a flat pan. A cat will lap it up. Pet a dog and put a leash on him. Take him up a hill and sit on the grass. Toss a stick and play. You can have a lot of fun and make a quick ten bucks.

When you get big, you must get a job. It is best to go to a trade school or a college. You can get skills to help you fix trucks, fill gas tanks, help a vet, or run a craft shop. You can help a kid add sums or help a sick kid get well. You can fly big and fast jets!

So get up and get dressed, and get a job!

B. **Read the passage again. Answer the following questions.**

1. What job can you do with pets?

   _____

2. What kind of job would you like?

   _____

 **Read the passage to a family member or a friend. Discuss the job he or she has now or what job he or she would like to have in the future. What skills are needed for this job?**

In a consonant blend, two or three consonants appear together. Each consonant sound is pronounced. The blend sometimes comes at the end of a word.

- The blend *nt* sounds like /n//t/, as in *plant*.
- The blend *nd* sounds like /n//d/, as in *band*.

A. Look at the pictures. Read the following words out loud. Circle the final blends.

band

pond

plant

B. Complete each sentence with a word from the box below. Then read the sentences out loud.

| band   pond   sand   send   tent   went |

1. Ann and Ben want to _____ a present to me.

2. My class _____ on a trip yesterday.

3. I had _____ in my shorts at the beach.

4. Min went to the _____ to see the ducks.

5. Nell plays the drums in the school _____.

6. We brought our _____ for camping.

C. Read the following paragraph out loud. Then underline the words with the final blends *nd* and *nt*.

   Our class went on a trip to the pond. We saw ducks swimming in the pond and sitting on the land.

   We had snacks, but we had to fend off the ants! We looked at a lot of plants. We got to hunt in the grass to find little bugs.

   Brent did a back flip in the sand. We sat on the dock in the sun and the wind. I did not want the trip to end.

Name _____ Date _____

FINAL BLENDS: *sp, st, sk, lt, ld*

In a consonant blend, two or three consonants appear together. Each consonant sound is pronounced. The blend sometimes comes at the end of a word.

- The blend *sp* sounds like /s//p/, as in *grasp*.
- The blend *st* sounds like /s//t/, as in *vest*.
- The blend *sk* sounds like /s//k/, as in *desk*.
- The blend *lt* sounds like /l//t/, as in *melt*.
- The blend *ld* sounds like /l//d/, as in *held*.

A. Look at the pictures. Read the following words out loud. Circle the final blends.

wasp   vest   desk

melt   old

B. Read the words out loud. Then write a rhyming word for each word.

1. brisk _____

2. best _____

3. weld _____

4. crisp _____

5. felt _____

6. mist _____

C. Complete each sentence with a word from the box below. Then read the sentences out loud.

clasp   desk   held   melt

1. Nick sits at this _____.

2. If that gets hot, it will _____.

3. Mom _____ the dog down for the vet.

4. The _____ on her bag was locked.

Chapter 2 • Consonant Blends

43

FINAL DIGRAPH: *ng;* FINAL BLEND: *nk*

Two letters making one sound is called a digraph. The /ng/ sound has two spellings: *n* and *ng*.

- The letters *ng* at the end of a word can sound like /ng/, as in *ring*.
- The letter *n* can sound like /ng/ when it is blended with *k* at the end of a word, as in *sink*.

A. Look at the pictures. Read the following words out loud. Circle the final blend or digraph.

ring

sink

B. Write as many words as you can using these endings.

1. __ang _____

2. __ing _____

3. __ung _____

4. __ank _____

5. __ink _____

6. __unk _____

C. Read the sentences out loud. Then underline the words with the digraph *ng* and circle the words with the blend *nk*.

1. Frank likes to sing songs.

2. Her pink socks stink.

3. Fill the truck's gas tank to the top.

4. The dog drank from the sink.

5. I will bring my mom a ring.

6. I had a long nap.

7. If you skip class, you will flunk.

CHAPTER 2 REVIEW

A. Circle the correct word to complete each sentence. Then read the sentences out loud.

1. We can (sled, slid, sledding) down the hill.

2. Jeff was the (list, last, lasted) to come.

3. Dad has to cut the (glass, grass, gloss).

4. I am (glad, clad, gladding) that you are well now.

5. Jan wants to (bring, bling, swing) the hot dog buns.

6. The (crib, crab, crack) is moving in the sand.

7. Where are you going on your (trap, trip, tip)?

8. The box is (flat, flap, fell) and long.

9. Pat (felt, fled, fed) sick at school.

10. The funny hat was (black, block, trick) and red.

B. Correct the underlined words. If the word is correct, put a check mark over it. Then read the paragraph out loud.

My class <u>plan</u> a big trip. We <u>rent</u> a van and a truck. We <u>pack</u> stuff like hats, tops, pots,
  1.   2.   3.

and snacks in the truck. We <u>went</u> west, to the Black Hills. Miss Ross let us <u>singing</u> funny
                              4.   5.

songs on the ride. At last, the ride <u>end</u>.
                                        6.

We <u>lug</u> the stuff off the truck. We <u>set</u> up a big tent in the soft grass. Miss Ross said,
    7.   8.

"<u>Looked</u> at the land and rocks makes one glad." She is funny like that. Still, we <u>felt</u> glad,
  9.   10.

just like she did.

CHAPTER 2 REVIEW (continued)

C. Fill in the chart below with two other words with the same initial blend.

speck spell **1.** spin spot	trick trap **2.** ________ ________	crack crib **3.** ________ ________	blink bland **4.** ________ ________	flag flip **5.** ________ ________
staff stuck **6.** ________ ________	grin grand **7.** ________ ________	prim prom **8.** ________ ________	cling clap **9.** ________ ________	pluck plot **10.** ________ ________

D. Read the following words out loud. Circle the words that have the same final blend or final digraph. Underline the blend or digraph. Then write your own word with the same ending.

1. sink sing wink link

2. wisp list last ________

3. melt belt weld ________

4. send sent land ________

5. lisp asp mist ________

CHAPTER 3   LONG VOWELS

Long *a*: *a_e*... 48

Short *a* and Long *a*: *a_e*....................... 49

Long *a*: *ay*.. 50

Long *a*: *ai* 51

Long *o*: *o_e*... 52

Short *o* and Long *o*: *o_e*...................... 53

Word Analysis: Inflections: *-ed, -ing* 54

Long *o*: *oa*.. 55

Long *o*: *ow*... 56

Long *o*: *o, oe*.. 57

High Frequency Words: Set 5 58

Reading Practice: Passage 5 59

Long *i*: *i_e*.. 60

Short *i* and Long *i*: *i_e* 61

Long *i*: *igh* 62

Long *i*: *ie*... 63

Long *i*: *y*... 64

Long *i*: *i* 65

Long *u*: *u_e*.. 66

Short *u* and Long *u*: *u_e* 67

Long *u*: *oo* 68

High Frequency Words: Set 6 69

Reading Practice: Passage 6 70

Long *e*: *ee*.. 71

Long *e*: *ea*.. 72

Short *e* and Long *e*: *ee, ea* 73

Long *e*: *ie* 74

Long *e*: *e* 75

Long *e*: *ey, y* 76

Word Analysis: Inflections: *-ed, -es, -ing* 77

High Frequency Words: Set 7 78

Reading Practice: Passage 7 79

Word Analysis:
CVCe Syllables and Phonograms 80

Word Analysis:
CVVC Syllables (Vowel Teams)............. 81

Chapter 3 Review................................ 82

Name _____ Date _____

The letter *a* can stand for the long vowel sound /ā/, as in *take*. When *a* is followed by a consonant and the letter *e*, the vowel sound is usually long. The *e* is usually silent.

A. Look at pictures. Write the letters to complete the words. Then read the words out loud.

__ __ ke

t __ __ __

__ __ te

B. Complete the following words with *a_e*. Then read the words out loud.

1. f__d__

2. s__m__

3. gr__d__

4. s__v__

C. Complete each sentence with a word from the box below.

date grade late name same skate

1. What is today's _____*date*_____?

2. What _____ did you get in this class?

3. Did you get the _____ grade as Hal?

4. I _____ at the ice rink.

5. Do not come to school _____.

6. How do you spell your _____?

Name _____ Date _____

SHORT *a* and LONG *a*: *a_e*

The letter *a* can stand for the short vowel sound /a/, as in *mad*. When *a* is followed by a consonant and the letter *e*, the vowel sound is usually long, as in *made*. The *e* is usually silent.

A. Look at the pictures. Write the letters to complete the words. Then read the words out loud.

c __ __

c __ __ __

B. Read the following words out loud. Draw lines to connect the words that rhyme.

pale   pal

rat   cap

mate   sale

tap   rate

cape   tape

Sal   mat

C. Circle the correct word to complete each sentence. Then read the sentences out loud.

1. What is the (rat, rate) to rent a car for a day?

2. Jim sang on the (stag, stage).

3. Where (can, cane) we go?

4. I want to buy (pats, plates).

5. We (cam, came) to school late.

6. That (plan, plane) has landed.

7. The (fat, fate) king ate all the bread.

LONG *a: ay*

The letters *ay* can stand for the long vowel sound /ā/, as in *stay*.

A. Look at the pictures. Write the letters to complete the words. Then read the words out loud.

p __ __ __   h __ __   cl __ __

B. Read the following sentences out loud. Circle the words that have the long vowel sound /a/ spelled *ay*.

1. Your drink is on the (tray.)

2. Did you say to go this way?

3. That dish is made of clay.

4. May I lay this on your desk?

5. The gray cat wants to stay here.

6. If you want to play in the band, just ask Ray.

C. Complete each sentence with a word from the box below. Then read the sentences out loud.

| day   may   pay   stay   sway   way |

1. The wind made the big tree _____*sway*_____.

2. Which _____ is payday?

3. We will have to _____ for the snacks.

4. Dave's dog will _____ in the back yard.

5. _____ I have something to drink?

6. Did he go that _____?

Name _____ Date _____

LONG _a_: _ai_

The letters _ai_ can stand for the long vowel sound /ā/, as in _drain_.

A. Look at the pictures. Write the letters to complete the words. Then read the words out loud.

t _ _ _ _   br _ _ d   sn _ _ _ _

B. Complete the following words with _ai_. Then read the words out loud.

1. l_____d   6. tr_____l

2. m_____d   7. m_____n

3. p_____d   8. p_____n

4. m_____l   9. dr_____n

5. n_____l   10. p_____nt

C. Complete the following sentences with a word from the box below. Then read the sentences out loud.

| brain fail mail paid rain tail train |

1. I _____ the lady for my lunch.

2. Your _____ is in your skull.

3. It's sunny today, but it will _____ tomorrow.

4. Mom got a box in the _____.

5. My dog wags his _____ when he is happy.

6. The _____ will get you here fast.

7. If you _____ the test, you can make it up.

LONG *o*: *o_e*

The letter *o* can stand for the long vowel sound /ō/, as in *pole*. When *o* is followed by a consonant and the letter *e*, the vowel sound is usually long. The *e* is usually silent.

A. Look at the pictures. Write the letters to complete the words. Then read the words out loud.

h __ m __   gl __ b __   h __ s __

B. Complete the following words with *o_e*. Then read the words out loud.

1. h__p__

2. n__t__

3. sl__p__

4. t__t__

5. r__d__

6. c__d__

C. Read the following letter out loud. Underline the words with long vowel sound /ō/ spelled *o_e*.

Dear Rose,

I hope you are well. I am sending you a note to tell you that I like the robe you sent me for my birthday. It arrived at my home yesterday. I can see that is was made in Rome! I will wear this robe every day. Now, I will call Tim. As a joke, he sent me a globe for my birthday!

Best wishes,

Cole

Name _____ Date _____

SHORT *o* and LONG *o*: *o_e*

The letter *o* can stand for the short vowel sound /o/, as in *pot*. When *o* is followed by a consonant and *e*, the vowel sound is usually long, as in *pole*. The *e* is usually silent.

A. Look at the pictures. Read the following words out loud. Circle the letters that stand for the short vowel sound /o/ and the long vowel sound /ō/.

tot

tote

B. Read the following words out loud. Fill in the chart with the correct words.

mope	code	cope	hop	rod	not
note	mop	cod	hope	cop	rode

Short vowel sound *o*	Long vowel sound *o*
cod	*code*

C. Complete each sentence with a word pair from the box below. Then read the sentences out loud.

hop/hope   not/note   Rob/robe   Sam/same

1. I _____*hope*_____ the frog did not _____*hop*_____ into the pond.

2. My mom will _____ get a _____ from Miss Hess.

3. _____ takes the _____ bus that I take.

4. _____ wore his _____ to bed.

WORD ANALYSIS: Inflections: -ed, -ing

Many base words end with *e*. When an *-ed* or *-ing* inflection is added, the final *e* is dropped from the base word. When the base word has a CVCe pattern, drop the final *e* and then add the inflection.

A. Read the examples in the box out loud. Then circle the inflection.

Base Word	*-ed*	*-ing*
save	saved	saving
hope	hoped	hoping

B. Complete the chart with the base word, *-ing* form, or *-ed* form of the word. Then read the words out loud.

Base Word	-ed	-ing
joke	_____	_____
_____	_____	baking
grade	graded	_____
vote	voted	_____
slope	_____	sloping
_____	coped	coping
race	_____	_____

C. Correct the underlined words in the following sentences. Write the words on the lines. Then read the sentences out loud.

1. I was <u>hopping</u> to see you here.   *hoping*

2. Jake <u>saveed</u> me from falling into the pond.   _____

3. We are always <u>jokeing</u> and laughing.   _____

4. I am <u>takking</u> the puppy home.   _____

5. My mom <u>votted</u> for a new mayor.   _____

6. She is <u>makeing</u> socks for the family.   _____

LONG *o*: *oa*

The letters *oa* can stand for the long vowel sound /ō/, as in *throat*.

A. Look at the pictures. Write the letters to complete the words. Then read the words out loud.

__ __ __ __   __ __ __ __   __ __ __ __

B. Read the following words out loud. Draw lines to connect words that rhyme.

croak	moat
road	soak
loan	foal
coat	toad
goal	groan

C. Read the following sentences out loud. Underline the words with the long vowel sound /ō/ spelled *oa*.

1. The toads at the pond croak all day.

2. I will use the soap when I soak in the tub.

3. Joan groaned when she dropped the pan.

4. I will boast that I scored a goal at the soccer game.

5. Mom made a delicious roast, and Dad made a long toast.

6. That boat will float in a terrible storm.

7. The goat ate his oats near the moat.

LONG *o*: *ow*

The letters *ow* can stand for the long vowel sound /ō/, as in *show*.

A. Look at the pictures. Write the letters to complete the words. Then read the words out loud.

b _ _ _   t _ _   g _ _ _

B. Complete the following words with *ow*. Then read the words out loud.

1. l_____   6. cr_____

2. m_____   7. fl_____

3. r_____   8. sn_____

4. s_____   9. b_____l

5. gr_____   10. _____n

C. Complete each sentence with a word from the box below. Then read the sentences out loud.

| blown   flown   flows   glows   grown   slowly |

1. The birds have _____*flown*_____ south for the winter.

2. Please drive _____. There are a lot of children in this neighborhood.

3. The flowers and plants have _____ very tall.

4. The campfire _____ in the dark.

5. The wind has _____ the bird's nest down.

6. That river _____ into the ocean.

LONG o: o, oe

The letter *o* can stand for the long vowel sound /ō/, as in *no*. The letters *oe* can also stand for the long vowel sound /ō/, as in *foe*.

A. Look at the pictures. Write the letters to complete the words. Then read the words out loud.

g __

h __ __

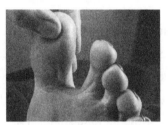

t __ __

B. Read the following sentences out loud. Circle the letters that stand for the long vowel sound /ō/.

1. No, I cannot go on that long trip.

2. Joe stubbed his toe.

3. It is so hot that I might go swimming.

4. The old farmer could work if he had a hoe.

5. Most foes won't go.

6. He goes for a stroll with Josie.

C. Read the following words out loud. Draw lines to connect the words that rhyme.

toad   cope

goes   coal

stale   coast

own   cane

main   bone

bowl   jail

soap   rose

most   road

A. You will see these ten words in many books. Read the words out loud.

blue	four	our	please	there	three	two	was	were	yellow

B. Read the following passage out loud. Then circle the high frequency words.

Jake's class was at camp. The yellow morning sun was up early. Soon after, Jake and Nell were awake. At camp, that day, there were two little frogs, three big toads, four old bucks, and one blue snake. The blue snake made Jake jump. The snake was still, sitting on his rock, so Jake came close to it.

"Please tell me that is not a snake," Jake said to Nell.

"It's okay," said Nell. "Just take a slow step back."

Jake stepped back.

"Now we have a tale to tell," said Nell. "This will be our tale of the blue snake."

"Yes," said Jake. "I can't wait to tell our friends!"

C. Read the passage again. Answer the following questions.

1. How many animals were at the camp? What were they?

   _____

2. What was Jake and Nell's tale about?

   _____

READING PRACTICE: Passage 5

A. Read the following passage out loud.

Playing a Game

Cole wanted to play a game. "Will you please play a game?" Cole asked his pals, Ann and Jim.

"I am up for a game. How is it played?" Ann asked.

Jim said, "Yes, I am in, too."

Cole told Ann and Jim, "The goal is to kick a tin can up to a net, and get it in. Two kids will block the net and one kid will kick the can in. It is a fun game."

Ann and Jim had big wide grins. "That can and net game will be fun, but how do you get a winner, and what is the name of this game?" they asked.

"To win, a kid must score ten goals, and the game's name is 'Kick the Can.'" Cole explained.

Ann, Jim, and Cole played "Kick the Can" that day and the next day as well.

B. Read the passage again. Answer the following questions.

1. What are the names of Cole's pals?

_____

2. How do you know the pals liked the game?

_____

Home-School Connection Read the passage to a family member or a friend. Discuss your favorite sports. Do you both like to play the same games?

LONG i: i_e

The letter *i* can stand for the long vowel sound /ī/. When *i* is followed by a consonant and the letter *e*, the vowel sound is usually long, as in *kite*. The *e* is usually silent.

A. Look at the pictures. Write the letters to complete the words. Then read the words out loud.

b __ __ __

sm __ l __

d __ __ __

B. Read the following words out loud. Find and circle the words.

hike   nine   smile   time   wipe

d	e	t	f	g	h
i	k	i	n	l	m
n	s	m	i	l	e
o	p	e	n	s	t
w	i	p	e	w	d
e	f	h	i	k	e

C. Circle the word with the long vowel sound /ī/ to complete each sentence. Then read the sentences out loud.

1. What (tin, tome, time) is it?

2. You will have to stand in (line, lint, lane) to get in.

3. We can make a warm (fit, fire, fist) in that pit.

4. Mike has a big (sill, smile, spell) and nice teeth.

5. I hiked (fun, fit, five) miles down that hill.

Chapter 3 • Long Vowels

SHORT *i* and LONG *i*: *i_e*

The letter *i* can stand for the short vowel sound /i/, as in *win*. When *i* is followed by a consonant and the letter *e*, the vowel sound is usually long, as in *vine*. The *e* is usually silent.

A. Look at the pictures. Write the letters to complete the words. Then read the words out loud.

tw __ ns

tw __ n __

B. Read the following words with the short vowel sound /i/ out loud. Add *e* to the end of the words to make words with the long vowel sound /ī/. Then write the word. Read the new words out loud.

1. hid _____*hide*_____   **6.** prim _____

2. dim _____   **7.** grim _____

3. bit _____   **8.** slim _____

4. quit _____   **9.** grip _____

5. fin _____   **10.** slid _____

C. Read the following sentences out loud. Circle the words with the short vowel sound /i/. Underline the words with long vowel sound /ī/.

1. (Tim) likes to ride (his) bike up and down (hills.)

2. That game was quite a bit of fun for him.

3. There are five pins in that cup.

4. Mike can help you win a prize.

5. I can sit on a rock and sniff the pines.

6. Jill spent ten dollars on this tire.

7. The sun will rise at six.

8. Sit still and write your lines.

LONG *i*: *igh*

The letters *igh* can stand for the long vowel sound /ī/, as in *tight*. The *gh* is silent.

A. Look at the pictures. Write the letters to complete the words. Then read the words out loud.

l __ __ __ t

n __ __ __ __

br __ __ __ t

B. Complete each sentence with a word from the box below. Then read the sentences out loud.

> fight   flight   high   right   sight   tight

1. Our _____ from Texas comes in at nine.

2. The jeans are too _____ for me.

3. I hope our kite will fly _____.

4. Ask Jane to tell us the _____ way to go.

5. The sunset was a beautiful _____.

6. Mom does not want us to _____ with each other.

C. Complete the words in the following sentences with the long vowel sound /ī/ spelled *igh*. Then read the sentences out loud.

1. At n _igh_ t, I like to look way up h _igh_ at the sky.

2. That br_____t l_____t is coming from his home.

3. On the r_____t, there is a sl_____t turn in the road.

4. I m_____t take a fl_____t to Rome.

5. I hope to get there r_____t on time, but I m_____t be late.

Name _____ Date _____

LONG i: ie

The letters *ie* can stand for the long vowel sound /ī/, as in *die*. The *e* is usually silent.

A. Look at the pictures. Write the letters to complete the words. Then read the words out loud.

— — —

— — —

B. Read the following words out loud. Underline the letters that stand for the long vowel sound /ī/.

1. lied   7. dries

2. lie   8. ties

3. pie   9. flies

4. tied   10. tried

5. cried   11. died

6. pried

C. Read the following sentences out loud. Circle the words that have the long vowel sound /ī/ spelled *ie*. Then write your own sentence using an *ie* word. Circle the *ie* word.

1. There were flies in the hut.

2. Do not tell a lie.

3. I had fried clams and pie.

4. We gave Dad a yellow and blue tie.

5. Tom tried to stay up late last night.

6. _____

LONG *i: y*

The letter *y* stands for the long vowel sound /ī/, as in *try*.

A. Look at the pictures. Write the letters to complete the words. Then read the words out loud.

— — —   — — —

B. Circle the word that has the long vowel sound /ī/ to complete each sentence. Then read the sentences out loud.

1. David will (fill, fail, (fly)) to Spain.

2. Will saw a big plane in the (scab, sky, sick).

3. Please step off of (my, me, am) coat so I can pick it up.

4. We (tree, true, try) to play chess.

5. He lives (be, by, big) the bus stop.

6. The (dry, drew, drip) air makes me ill.

C. Complete each sentence with a word from the box below. Then read the sentences out loud.

by cry dry my sky try

1. The floor is _____ *dry* _____ now.

2. Is the _____ blue or gray?

3. The store is right _____ the school.

4. Jake will _____ to get to school on time.

5. Please come to _____ house for dinner tonight.

6. The baby doesn't _____ at night anymore.

Name _____ Date _____

LONG *i: i*

The letter *i* can stand for the long vowel sound /ī/, as in *wild*.

A. Look at the pictures. Write the letters to complete the words. Then read the words out loud.

w __ nd   bl __ __ d   __ __ __ ld

B. Complete the following words with the long vowel sound /ī/. Then read the words out loud.

1. b__nd

2. f__nd

3. k__nd

4. m__ld

5. gr__nd

6. p__nt

C. Complete each sentence with a word from the box below. Then read the sentences out loud.

find   hind   kind   mild   mind   wind

1. What _____ of dog do you have?

2. Please _____ up the jack-in-the-box for Tim.

3. The day was _____ and bright.

4. Where can we _____ a nice place to eat?

5. I do not _____ making the bed.

6. The goat's _____ legs kicked Gus.

Long Vowels • Chapter 3

LONG *u: u_e*

The letter *u* can stand for the long vowel sound /ū/, as in *prune*. When *u* is followed by a consonant and the letter *e*, the vowel sound is usually long. The *e* is usually silent.

A. Look at the pictures. Write the letters to complete the words. Then read the words out loud.

fl __ t __   m __ l __   c __ b __

B. Read the following words out loud. Draw lines to connect the words that rhyme.

rude	cure
rule	plume
fume	dude
pure	flute
June	mule
cute	tune

C. Circle the words that have the long /u/ sound to complete each sentence. Then read the sentences out loud.

1. I play the ((flute), flunk, punt) in the school band.

2. May I (fuss, fun, use) your bat and mitt?

3. June can play a (ton, tune, tub) on the flute.

4. The (cut, cute, cup) cub was in his den.

5. Matt made a (cube, cub, can) shape with his clay.

6. That baby is so (cut, cute, cup).

Name _____ Date _____

SHORT *u* and LONG *u*: *u_e*

The letter *u* can stand for the short vowel sound /u/, as in *tub*. When *u* is followed by a consonant and the letter *e*, the vowel sound is usually long, as in *tube*. The *e* is usually silent.

A. Look at the pictures. Write the letters to complete the words. Then read the words out loud.

c __ b

c __ b __

B. Complete the following sentences with a word pair from the box below. Then read the sentences out loud.

cut/cute   hug/huge   tub/tube   us/use

1. Jess ___*cut*___ up a box to make a house for his ___*cute*___ pet rabbit.

2. Ms. Hoff helps _____ try to _____ the class time wisely.

3. Dad gave me a _____ _____ when I came home.

4. A hose is a long _____ you can use to fill up a _____ with water.

C. Read the words below out loud. Then write the words in the correct column. Some words do not belong in the chart. Leave them out.

blank   bunk   crude   cub   cute   dude   flunk   flute

mule   plum   pure   smug   stem   stun   tube   tune

Words with Short Vowel Sound /u/	Words with Long Vowel Sound /ū/
plum	*dude*

LONG *u*: *oo*

The letters *oo* can stand for the long vowel sound /ū/, as in *tool*.

A. Look at the pictures. Write the letters to complete the words. Then read the words out loud.

f __ __ __   br __ __ m   sp __ __ __

B. Read the following words out loud. Then write a rhyming word that contains the long vowel sound /ū/ spelled *oo*.

1. proof   _____*roof*_____

2. pool   _____

3. mood   _____

4. bloom   _____

5. troop   _____

6. boot   _____

C. Complete each sentence with a word from the box below.

groom   moon   noon   pool   roof   tool   troops

1. Use the right _____ for the job.

2. Bring the _____ home safe.

3. The bride and _____ ate the cake.

4. At _____, our class will end.

5. The _____ is bright at night.

6. We can go swimming in the _____.

7. The crow is sitting on the _____.

         Chapter 3 • Long Vowels

HIGH FREQUENCY WORDS: Set 6

A. You will see these ten words in many books. Read the words out loud.

| away | could | give | her | new | put | these | those | who | with |

B. Read the following passage out loud. Then circle the high frequency words.

I went to the store to buy new boots. My friend Jane works there. I put on a pair of blue boots, but in a size four. The left one felt okay, but the right one was kind of tight.

"Could I try these in a size five?" I said to her. "And, could you bring me those yellow boots, too?"

I gave the tight boots back. Jane put them back on the shelf.

Soon, she came back with the yellow boots and the blue boots in a size five.

"These boots fit well," I said to her. "I will take the blue boots and the yellow boots. How much do they cost"

"Ten dollars," said Jane.

"Thanks, Jane," I said.

C. Read the passage again. Answer the following questions.

1. Who works at the shoe store?

_____

2. What size boots did the woman buy?

_____

Long Vowels • Chapter 3

A. Read the following passage out loud.

A Bright Day

I like swimming. Ken, Lane, and Ray like swimming, too. Our school has a big new pool, so we are glad. We can join the swimming club. The swimming club kids can take a bus to other schools. Ken, Lane, Ray, and I swim and dive to win prizes.

Kids in my class like to run track. Kids that run track can run and jump and sprint. The track club kids take a bus to other schools, and the kids run with each other. They run, jump, and sprint to win prizes.

Kids in my class like to tap dance. The tap club kids take a bus and tap for folks who are sick or just need a pal. They tap, tap, tap, and the folks smile and say, "Thank you for making my day brighter."

So join a club. You can make pals, smile a lot, and help sick folks have a bright day.

B. Read the passage again. Answer the following questions.

1. What does the school have?

_____

2. What does the school not have?

_____

Read the passage to a family member or a friend. Does that person belong to any clubs or groups? Do you? Discuss the kinds of clubs and groups at your school.

Chapter 3 • Long Vowels

LONG *e: ee*

The letters *ee* can stand for the long vowel sound /ē/, as in *meet*.

A. Look at the pictures. Write the letters to complete the words. Then read the words out loud.

— — —   — — — —

B. Read the following sentences out loud. Then circle the words that have the long vowel sound /ē/ spelled *ee*.

1. Can you see those green trees?

2. Lee will sit next to me at the meeting.

3. The queen ate a lot of sweets.

4. I cannot sleep unless I keep a light on.

5. Have you seen Dee lately?

C. Complete each sentence with a word from the box below. Then read the sentences out loud.

| feet   free   see   seeds   sixteen   sweep |

1. You can _____ for miles if you hike to the top of that hill.

2. She will be _____ years old in just two weeks.

3. Please _____ the living room, and I will mop in the kitchen.

4. My _____ are too big to fit in your boots.

5. We let the fox that was stuck in that trap go _____.

6. We plant little _____ to grow mighty trees.

LONG *e: ea*

The letters *ea* can stand for the long vowel sound /ē/, as in *clean*.

A. Look at the pictures. Write the letters to complete the words. Then read the words out loud.

b __ __ k

__ __ __ d

B. Read the following sentences out loud. Underline the words that have *ea*. Circle the words that have *ee*.

1. Can you make a ring with these red and green beads?

2. If we meet, please do not sneak up on me.

3. Let me read at least two or three pages.

4. I will eat veal, and I will have sweet peas and beans.

5. I keep my room neat, and I like to sweep it clean once a week.

C. Answer each riddle with a word from the box below. Then read each riddle out loud.

beach   flea   tree

I am very tall and green.
You can pick a leaf off me.
What am I?

_____

I have sand and waves.
You can visit me by the sea.
What am I?

_____

Cats and dogs scratch at me.
You may need to get rid of me.
What am I?

_____

SHORT *e* and LONG *e*: *ee, ea*

The letter *e* can stand for the short vowel sound /e/, as in *bed*. The letters *ee* and *ea* can stand for the long vowel sound /ē/, as in *seem* and *team*.

A. Look at the pictures. Write the letters to complete the words. Then read the words out loud.

t __ n

t __ __ n

t __ __ m

B. Circle the correct word to complete each sentence. Then read the sentences out loud.

1. I like to eat (oatmeal, oatmeel, oatmell).

2. Jean got (wet, weat, weet) with the hose.

3. We need (tean, ten, teen) men to roll that truck.

4. There was one (been, ben, bean) left on her plate.

5. It was difficult for our (teem, tem, team) to win the game.

C. Read the following words out loud. Write the words in the correct column. Some words do not belong in the chart. Leave them out.

beach	bead	beat	bed	bee	bet	flat	flea
flee	fun	hen	jet	meal	men	read	seat
set	spoon	sweet	tea	ten	tent	treat	wet

Short Vowel Sound /e/	**Long Vowel Sound /ē/**
bet	bee

LONG e: *ie*

The letters *ie* can stand for the long vowel sound /ē/, as in *puppies*.

A. Look at the pictures. Write the letters to complete the words. Then read the words out loud.

f __ __ ld

y __ __ ld

br __ __ fcase

B. Complete the following words with the long vowel sound /ē/ spelled *ie*. Then read the words out loud.

1. br_____f

2. bab_____s

3. f_____ld

4. y_____ld

5. famil_____s

C. Read the following sentences out loud. Underline the words that have the long vowel sound /ē/ spelled *ie*.

1. We have gym class on the field unless it rains.

2. There is a yield sign by the school.

3. Ms. Lee needs to speak briefly to our class.

4. James felt deep grief when he lost his dog.

5. In the fifties and sixties Martin Luther King Jr., led rallies for our rights.

Name _____ Date _____

The letter *e* can stand for the long vowel sound /ē/, as in *detour*. The syllable with the long vowel sound /ē/ is usually stressed.

A. Look at the pictures. Write the letters to complete the words. Then read the words out loud.

        f __ line   r __ lay

B. Read the following words out loud. Then circle the long vowel sound /ē/.

1. me

2. begin

3. he

4. we

5. beyond

6. rerun

C. Complete each sentence with a word from the box below. Then read the sentences out loud.

be   me   reruns   reset   retake   she

1. Kate's mom said _____ could drive us to the basketball game.

2. We will have to _____ our clocks for daylight saving time.

3. Will you please hand _____ that nail?

4. If I fail the test today, I can _____ it next week.

5. Where will you _____ at five o'clock?

6. I do not like to watch _____ on TV.

LONG e: ey, y

The letters *ey* and *y* can stand for the long vowel sound /ē/, as in *monkey* and *happy*.

A. Look at the pictures. Write the letters to complete the words. Then read the words out loud.

k __ __ s   dais __   all __ __

B. Read the following words out loud. Then circle the letters that stand for the long vowel sound /ē/.

1. body	**5.** study	**9.** daily
2. copy	**6.** key	**10.** Sally
3. very	**7.** tiny	**11.** sunny
4. funny	**8.** valley	**12.** paisley

C. Complete each sentence with a word from the box below. Then read the sentences out loud.

alley happy key lucky valleys very

1. In this game the _____*lucky*_____ one wins, not the one with the best skills.

2. I need a _____ to open the lock.

3. Abby is _____ that tomorrow is her birthday.

4. A snake can be _____ still.

5. Go through the _____ to go in the back way.

6. We will go up hills and down _____ on our road trip.

WORD ANALYSIS: Inflections: -ed, -es, -ing

When adding an inflection to a base word ending in *y*, change the *y* to an *i* before adding the inflections *-ed* and *-es*. When adding the inflection *-ing*, there is no change.

A. Read the following words out loud. Circle the inflections.

Base Word	-ed	-es	-ing
study	studied	studies	studying
spy	spied	spies	spying
deny	denied	denies	denying

B. Complete the chart with the base word, -ed form, -es form, or -ing form of the word. Then read the words out loud.

Base Word	-ed	-es	-ing
worry	_____	worries	_____
try	_____	tries	_____
cry	_____	_____	crying
_____	dried	_____	drying
fry	fried	_____	_____

C. Correct the spelling of the underlined words in the following paragraph. Then read the paragraph out loud.

I am <u>studing</u> how to fly a plane. I will try to make <u>fliing</u> my job when I grow up. As
    1.   2.

a jet or a plane <u>flyes</u> by, I look up in the blue <u>skyes</u> and dream. There is no <u>denyying</u> it, I
               3.   4.   5.

really want to fly.

A. You will see these ten words in many books. Read the words out loud.

after	always	because	done	from	going	how	or	under	when

B. Read the following passage out loud. Then circle the high frequency words.

When the day is done, it is time to get in bed and sleep. You don't always have dreams when you sleep. There are at least two stages of sleep: REM and deep sleep. Just after going to bed, you nod off to sleep. That is when you go into the state of REM sleep. REM sleep is when we dream. After REM sleep, we go into the deep sleep state. No one can tell how we go from one sleep stage to the next.

Dreams can tell us when we are under stress or are upset. That is because our dreams come from the experiences of our days. When you have a dream, here is what you can do to help you remember them: After you wake up from your dream, always write it down. Then you can read it the next day and think about what your dream might mean.

C. Read the passage again. Answer the following questions.

1. In what stage of sleep do you dream?

   _____

2. What can you do to help you remember your dreams?

   _____

READING PRACTICE: Passage 7

A. Read the following passage out loud.

Our May Project

My class is going to clean up the playing field at our school. It is our May project. We do this every year. This Friday, when we are done with our classes, we will all meet on the field with plastic bags and tools from home. We will all bring our rakes and hoes.

There is a lot to do. We will pick up the junk that kids have dropped. After we tidy up, we are going to rake the grass and plant pansies and daisies. Then it will look beautiful.

We want to do this project because we want to make plain how we feel. We like our school. We are proud of our school, too. Your class can do a project too!

B. Read the passage again. Answer the following questions.

1. What is the class going to clean up?

   _____

2. Why does the class want to do this project?

   _____

 Read the passage to a family member or a friend. Discuss ways you can keep your neighborhood or play fields clean and neat.

WORD ANALYSIS: CVCe Syllables and Phonograms

Many words have the consonant-vowel-consonant-silent *e* pattern or CVCe syllable pattern, such as *make*. Rhyming CVCe words are in the same word families — they share phonograms. A phonogram is a letter or set of letters that stand for a single sound, for example, *-ake*.

A. Read the following words out loud. Circle the CVCe syllable pattern in each word. Then write the word family.

date late skate	dine mine spine	mole pole stole	dune June prune	lane mane plane

B. Read the following sentences out loud. Circle the words with the CVCe syllable pattern.

1. (Jane) went to bed (late) last night.

2. We like to smell the pine trees at Gram's home.

3. There are nine of us going out to dine tonight.

4. Mike forgave Pete for selling his bike.

5. Jake gave Dane a bike to ride in the race.

6. Steve rises at five, but Dave gets up at nine.

C. Complete the chart with a rhyming word for each word family.

-ame	-ope	-ive	-use
came _lame_	mope _____	five _____	muse _____
-ade	**-one**	**-ide**	**-ule**
wade _____	bone _____	side _____	yule _____

Chapter 3 • Long Vowels

WORD ANALYSIS: CVVC Syllables (Vowel Teams)

Some words have the consonant-vowel-vowel-consonant pattern, or CVVC syllable pattern. A vowel team is two vowels that appear together and have one sound. Vowel teams often have a long vowel sound.

A. Read the following words out loud. Circle the vowel teams

Long /a/ Vowel Sound	Long /e/ Vowel Sound	Long /e/ Vowel Sound	Long /o/ Vowel Sound
pail	read	deep	road
laid	clean	peel	loan
rain	steam	feet	boat

B. Read the following words out loud. Draw lines to connect the words that rhyme. Then circle the vowel team for each pair.

1. meal   lone

2. treat   rode

3. mail   green

4. read   sweet

5. keep   greed

6. moan   sale

7. mean   feel

8. toad   reap

C. Complete each sentence with a word from the box below. Then read the sentences out loud.

> beans   coat   seed   sweep   tie   train

1. Jean had to _____*sweep*_____ the store.

2. Greg planted the _____ in the field by the tree.

3. Jill got a new _____ for winter.

4. She had green _____ with her meal.

5. We are going to take the _____ to Alaska.

6. _____ the laces on your hiking boots tight.

Long Vowels • Chapter 3

A. Circle the correct word to complete each sentence. Then read the sentences out loud.

1. I (mad/~~made~~) my mom a cake.

2. I (hope/hop) she liked her birthday gift.

3. "(Try/Tray) it!" I said. "I made it myself."

4. "This is fantastic," said Mom, as she (poked/pocked) at the icing.

5. Mom (at/ate) a bit of the cake and left the rest.

6. "Don't you (like/lick) the cake?" I asked.

7. "Yes, I do. But I will (at/eat) it after I've had a real meal."

8. "It was (sweet/sweat) of you to make that cake," Mom smiled.

9. Then she asked me to (clean/clip) up the mess.

10. Moms can be so (mean/men) sometimes!

B. Correct the spelling of the underlined words in the following paragraph. Then read the paragraph out loud.

Late last <u>nite</u> I was under my quilt. My <u>windoe</u> was banging on the <u>sied</u> of our <u>hoem</u>
     1.   2.   3.   4.

<u>kepeing</u> me from <u>sleaping</u>. I <u>sloly</u> got out of bed. The wind was <u>bloing</u> hard. The tall <u>pien</u>
  5.   6.   7.   8.   9.

<u>trey</u> in the back yard was moving back and forth. I <u>tryed</u> to <u>cloas</u> the <u>windoe</u>, but it was
 10.   11.   12.   13.

stuck. Just then, I got a <u>frite</u> when my cat jumped up on the window sill. Smack! Down
                  14.

<u>caim</u> the <u>windoe</u>, but that fast <u>feeline</u>, the best of the <u>tabbys</u>, was well on her <u>wai</u> to the
 15.   16.   17.   18.   19.

<u>ally</u> by then. Back in bed, I blinked <u>twyce</u> and went <u>rite</u> to a <u>nyce</u> <u>dreem</u>.
 20.   21.   22.   23.   24.

Name _____ Date _____

C. Complete each sentence by add *-ing, -ed, -es,* or *-ing* to the word in parentheses. Then read the sentences out loud.

1. It began to rain, so I _____*closed*_____ the window. (close)

2. I was _____ for a test when my cell rang. (study)

3. We are _____ from way back in the old days. (buddy)

4. I like to eat _____ clams when we visit Cape Cod. (fry)

5. We can pick _____ and make a pie when we get home. (blackberry)

6. The flight to Spain _____ daily from New York. (fly)

7. Mom _____ to smile, but she was sad when I went to camp. (try)

8. I hope she is not _____ when I get home! (cry)

9. I am _____ the window until it is very clean. (wipe)

10. She _____ hide and seek with her friends yesterday. (play)

D. Read the following words out loud. Find and circle the words.

ate   dune   rain   rode   soon   wade

cried   load   rent   snow   speed   wipe

f	s	n	o	w	c	w
d	u	n	e	a	r	i
r	e	n	t	d	i	p
r	a	i	n	e	e	e
l	o	a	d	i	d	c
r	o	d	e	u	e	e
s	p	e	e	d	t	s
s	o	o	n	d	a	s

CHAPTER 4   CONTRACTIONS AND CONSONANT DIGRAPHS

Word Analysis: Contractions with *not* 86

Word Analysis: Contractions with *will* 87

Word Analysis: Contractions with *would* 88

Word Analysis: Contractions with *have* 89

Word Analysis: Contractions with *are* 90

Word Analysis: Contractions with *is* 91

Word Analysis: Contractions
    with *'s* and Possessive *'s* 92

High Frequency Words: Set 8 93

Reading Practice: Passage 8 94

Initial Digraph: *th* 95

Final Digraph: *th* 96

Initial Digraph: *sh* 97

Final Digraph: *sh* 98

Initial Digraph: *ch* 99

Final Digraph: *ch;* Letters: *tch* 100

Initial Digraph: *wh* 101

Word Analysis: Inflections: *-er, -est* 102

High Frequency Words: Set 9 103

Reading Practice: Passage 9 104

Chapter 4 Review 105

WORD ANALYSIS: Contractions with *not*

A contraction is a single word made by combining two words. For example, the contraction *can't* is made by combining *can* and *not*. A contraction has an apostrophe (') to show where a letter or letters have been replaced.

A. Read the following contractions out loud. Circle the letter that the apostrophe replaces.

will not = **won't**	do not = **don't**	are not = **aren't**
did not = **didn't**	is not = **isn't**	cannot = **can't**
have not = **haven't**	does not = **doesn't**	must not = **mustn't**

B. Complete each sentence with a contraction. Then read the sentences out loud.

1. I _____*don't*_____ (do not) go to school on Sundays.

2. Blain _____ (will not) eat beets.

3. Shelly _____ (cannot) tell a crow from a robin.

4. I _____ (have not) told Sally that I like her bike.

5. Gail _____ (is not) meeting us in the park.

6. Her dress _____ (does not) hang down past her toes.

7. You _____ (must not) get wet, because there is no time to dry off.

8. Fred and Lin _____ (are not) going to pass this class if they

   _____ (do not) study.

C. Read the following sentences out loud. Underline the contractions. Then rewrite the sentences using the two words.

1. Don't play with her if she wasn't nice to you.

2. I can't do it, so I won't do it.

_____

_____

Name _____ Date _____

The word *will* can be used in contractions. The contraction *I'll* is made by combining *I* and *will*. The two words are joined with an apostrophe ('), which takes the place of the letters *wi*.

A. Read the following contractions out loud. Circle the letters that the apostrophe replaces.

I will = **I'll**	he will = **he'll**	we will = **we'll**
you will = **you'll**	she will = **she'll**	they will = **they'll**
	it will = **it'll**	

B. Complete each sentence with a contraction using *will* and the word in parentheses. Then read the sentences out loud.

1. Give the present to me and _____*I'll*_____ take it to Todd. (I)

2. _____ be glad to get the present from us. (He)

3. First, _____ see what is inside. (we)

4. _____ be fun to see what is inside. (It)

5. Maybe _____ win a radio. (she)

6. _____ see for yourself if he is happy or not. (You)

C. Correct the spelling of the underlined words. If the word is correct, put a check mark over it. Then read the paragraph out loud.

Penny is visiting us soon. <u>Shel'l</u> bring her cat, Dots, with her. <u>Theyll</u> get here by taking
                                                    1.   2.

the train. <u>Shell</u> have a seat and <u>heel</u> be in a big box with a tight lid. I like that cat. I hope
             3.   4.

<u>it'l</u> sleep on my bed. <u>I'll</u> let Dots sleep on my feet. That way <u>the'll</u> be toasty all night long.
5.   6.   7.

The next day <u>Ill</u> play with Penny. <u>We'l</u> play hide and seek and kick the can. Mom and Dad
                       8.   9.

will stay inside. <u>They'ill</u> make snacks for us to eat.
               10.

WORD ANALYSIS: Contractions with *would*

The word *would* can be used in contractions. The contraction *she'd* is made by combining *she* and *would*. The two words are joined with an apostrophe ('), which takes the place of the letters *woul*.

A. Read the following contractions out loud. Circle the letters that the apostrophe replaces.

I would = **I'd**	he would = **he'd**	we would = **we'd**
you would = **you'd**	she would = **she'd**	they would = **they'd**
	it would = **it'd***	

* *It'd* is used only in spoken language.

B. Complete each sentence with a contraction using *would* and the word in parentheses. Then read the sentences out loud.

1. _____ like to visit the zoo one day. (I)

2. If mom took us, _____ have to drive. (she)

3. _____ have a fun time. (We)

4. _____ enjoy seeing the seals. (She)

5. Animals need our help. At times, _____ die if we didn't help them. (they)

C. Correct the spelling of the underlined words. If the word is correct, put a check mark over it. Then read the paragraph out loud.

<u>I'd</u> _____ like to live under the sea. <u>Itw'd</u> _____ be neat to be with
1. 2.

the crabs and eels. <u>They'wd</u> _____ swim with me, and <u>Id</u> _____ have
3. 4.

to swim fast to keep up. <u>Youw'd</u> _____ like it too. <u>W'ed</u> _____ be quite
5. 6.

happy in the sea.

WORD ANALYSIS: Contractions with *have*

The word *have* can be used in contractions. The contraction *I've* is made by combining *I* and *have*. The two words are joined with an apostrophe ('), which takes the place of the letters *ha*.

A. Read the following contractions out loud. Circle the letters that the apostrophe replaces.

I have = **I've**	we have = **we've**
you have = **you've**	they have = **they've**

B. Complete each sentence with a contraction using *have* and the word in parentheses. Then read the sentences out loud.

1. _____*I've*_____ just seen a very big blue jay! (I)

2. I don't think _____ received their grades. (they)

3. _____ got to run fast if we are going to beat Matt. (We)

4. _____ got to get us to school on time. (They)

5. _____ a big lead in the art contest. (You)

6. I think _____ passed the exit. (we)

C. Correct the spelling of the underlined words. If the word is correct, put a check mark over it. Then read the letter out loud.

Maisy,

For a long time now, <u>Ive</u> wanted to tell you <u>you've</u> got a beautiful husky. <u>Iv'e</u> asked
                                   1.   2.   3.

Mom and Dad, and <u>they've</u> said that I can get a puppy. <u>We'ave</u> been to a few pet stores, but
                                 4.   5.

<u>Ive'</u> yet to find a husky like yours. Do you mind me asking what kind of husky you own?
 6.

I'd really like to get the same kind.

Yours truly,

Jane

WORD ANALYSIS: Contractions with *are*

The word *are* can be used in contractions. The contraction *we're* is made by combining *we* and *are*. The two words are joined with an apostrophe ('), which takes the place of the letter *a*.

A. Read the following contractions out loud. Circle the letter that the apostrophe replaces.

you are = **you're**	we are = **we're**	they are = **they're**

B. Complete each sentence by circling the correct contraction. Then read the sentences out loud.

1. Terry, (you're / we're) my best friend.

2. (We're / They're) going to the game tonight. Dad can take us.

3. Minnie's bowling club will sell painted bowling pins. (They're / We're) going to run an ad in the *School Times*.

4. (You're / We're) sad to see her go, aren't you?

5. I don't like peanuts because (they're / we're) too messy to eat.

6. Dad and I are happy. (We're / You're) going to make a little grass hut for my pet snake.

7. After Lee and Maddie get well, (you're / they're) taking a trip to Graceland.

C. Look again at the contractions you circled in Exercise B. Write the two words that each contraction stands for.

1. _____*you*_____   _____*are*_____

2. _____   _____

3. _____   _____

4. _____   _____

5. _____   _____

6. _____   _____

7. _____   _____

WORD ANALYSIS: Contractions with *is*

The word *is* can be used in contractions. The two words are joined with an apostrophe
('), which takes the place of the letter *i*.

A. Read the following contractions out loud. Circle the letter that the apostrophe replaces.

he is = **he's**	she is = **she's**	it is = **it's**
that is = **that's**	what is = **what's**	mom is = **mom's**

B. Complete each sentence with a contraction using is and the word in parentheses. Then read the sentences out loud.

1. Mr. Simms is my boss. _____*He's*_____ the nicest boss I've ever had. (He)

2. _____ my pen. Not yours! (That)

3. This book is very interesting. _____ a murder mystery. (It)

4. I can't wait to tell Mindy. _____ going to be very happy for me. (She)

5. Hey, Mom! _____ for dinner? (What)

6. Jenny's mom is taking us to school. My _____ picking us up. (mom)

7. _____ going to faint when he sees my grades. (He)

C. Complete each sentence by circling the correct contraction. Then read the paragraph out loud.

Ted: Look what I have, Mom!

Mom: ((What's)/ That's) this?
        1.

Ted: (He's / It's) my quiz. Look at that A.
      2.

Mom: (She's / That's) the best grade you can get!
      3.

Ted: No, (it's / he's) not. Next time I will get an A plus!
      4.

Mom: (That's / What's) a fine goal, but (he's / it's) not a big deal.
      5.   6.

An apostrophe is used to form contractions. In a contraction with *is*, the apostrophe takes the place of the letter *i*.

> **Tom's** a fast runner. (**Tom is** a fast runner.)

An apostrophe is also used to show possession.

> **Tom's** dog ran away. (**The dog that belongs to Tom** ran away.)

Possessive pronouns also show possession. Do not use an apostrophe with a possessive pronoun.

> CORRECT: The coat is **hers**. (INCORRECT: The coat is her's.)
> CORRECT: The pencil is **yours**. (INCORRECT: The pencil is your's.)
> CORRECT: The dog licked **its** paw. (INCORRECT: The dog licked it's paw.)

Never form a plural with an apostrophe.

> CORRECT: The **boys** came home. (INCORRECT: The boy's came home.)
> CORRECT: The **cats** are outside. (INCORRECT: The cat's are outside.)

A. Rewrite the following paragraph. Correct the contractions and possessives. Then read the paragraph out loud.

Its a sunny day. A dog licks it's tail by the gate. Dannys dog, Benny, like's to go visiting. As soon as the gate swing's open, Benny's off and running. The kids on the block like his' visits.

_____

_____

_____

_____

_____

Name _____ Date _____

A. You will see these ten words in many books. Read the words out loud.

about again buy found full goes language laugh their would

B. Read the following passage out loud. Then circle the high frequency words.

Would you like to learn another language? You can buy the DVD *Laugh and Study* to help you. Most of their DVDs are on sale right now, so you can get a good price. The man in the program will make you laugh. He tells stories about his funny experiences. He has one joke about how NOT to speak. He tells this joke with his mouth full of food. He also tells how he lost his dog and found it again. He goes into the city with his dog but loses him on the subway. Later he finds the little dog in the hat he is wearing! If you want to laugh again and again, buy this language DVD.

C. Read the passage again. Answer the following questions.

1. What's the name of the language DVD?

_____

2. Where does the man in the program find his dog?

_____

A. Read the following passage out loud.

Rise and Shine

Tad's clock rings at six o'clock. He does not mind getting right up. In the next room, Jean is still sleeping. She is a late-to-bed, late-to-wake-up type.

Mom is taking care of the new baby. He is just ten weeks old. Mom needs a lot of help right now. It is Tad's job to help out and see that he and Jean get to school on time.

"Rise and shine, sleepyhead. We will be late!"

"No, we will not be late!"

"Yes, we will be late," says Tad. "Come on and let's eat breakfast. We have eggs, wheat toast, and milk. We need a meal for energy."

"I am not hungry. I am still sleepy. Go away," Jean mumbles from under a quilt.

Tad and Jean say this day after day. Day after day for ten weeks, it is always the same.

B. Read the passage again. Answer the following questions.

1. What time does Tad wake up?

   _____

2. What do Tad and Jean say day after day?

   _____

 Read the passage to a family member or a friend. Does that person have any jobs at home? Do you? Discuss how you help out at home.

INITIAL DIGRAPH: *th*

The digraph *th* can stand for two sounds: /th/, as in *thumb* and /th̸/, as in *then*. The digraph *th* often appears at the beginning of a word.

A. Look at the pictures. Write the letters to complete the words. Then read the words out aloud.

__ __ ief

__ __ igh

__ __ ere

B. Read the following words out loud. Then write *TH* for /th̸/ or *th* for /th/ after each word.

1. the _____*TH*_____

2. thing _____

3. they'll _____

4. thin _____

5. think _____

6. there _____

7. thick _____

8. then _____

9. thank _____

10. them _____

11. three _____

12. those _____

C. Complete each sentence with a word from the box below. Then read the sentences out loud.

| thank   then   thing   think   thirsty   this |

1. I want to _____*thank*_____ you for the gift.

2. _____ game is the best one yet!

3. The _____ that I like best about Billy is that he is funny.

4. The rain stopped, but _____ it started again.

5. After running on the hot beach, I became very _____.

6. It's important to _____ clearly when you take a test.

FINAL DIGRAPH: *th*

The digraph *th* can stand for the sound /th/, as in *bath*. The digraph *th* often appears at the end of a word.

A. Look at the pictures. Write the letters to complete the words. Then read the words out loud.

clo __ __

tee __ __

mo __ __

B. Read the following words out loud. Then write a rhyming word for each.

1. booth _____

2. moth _____

3. path _____

4. breath _____

5. Ruth _____

C. Complete each sentence with a word from the box below. Then read the sentences out loud.

bath both broth cloth math moth teeth with

1. _____ *Broth* _____ can be made by boiling vegetables and meat.

2. _____ is my favorite class.

3. That dirty dog needs a _____.

4. I am here _____ my dad.

5. _____ of us want to see this film.

6. It's important to brush your _____ often.

7. That blue and yellow _____ is made of silk.

8. A _____ chewed a big hole in my new sweater.

Name _____ Date _____

The digraph *sh* stands for the sound /sh/, as in *show*. The digraph *sh* often appears at the beginning of a word.

A. Look at the pictures. Write the letters to complete the words. Then read the words out loud.

_ _ e _ p   _ _ ell   _ _ i _

B. Complete the following words by adding *sh*. Then read the words out loud.

1. ___*sh*__ in   5. _____ape   9. _____ade

2. _____ine   6. _____op   10. _____ampoo

3. _____ift   7. _____eet   11. _____ut

4. _____ame   8. _____iny   12. _____ave

C. Complete each sentence with a word from the box below. Then read the sentences out loud.

| shake   sheep   shelf   shell   shining   ship   shot   show |

1. That _____*shelf*_____ can hold a lot of things, but it needs to be wiped down.

2. Please don't _____ the can of soda!

3. His doctor gave him a _____ so that he wouldn't get the mumps.

4. I will _____ you how to make this cake. It's easy.

5. The sun was _____ this morning, but now it's cloudy.

6. I picked up a pink _____ from the sand.

7. The _____ almost sank during the storm.

8. They keep goats and _____ on their land.

FINAL DIGRAPH: *sh*

The digraph *sh* stands for the sound /sh/, as in *dish*. The digraph *sh* often appears at the end of a word.

A. Look at the pictures. Write the letters to complete the words. Then read the words out aloud.

b _ _ _ _   f _ _ _   ca _ _

B. Read the following words out loud. Draw lines to connect words that rhyme.

lash	brush
fish	posh
mesh	crash
gosh	wish
hush	fresh

C. Complete each sentence with a word from the box below. Then read the sentences out loud.

brush cash finish fishing push splash trash wish

1. Dad will _____*finish*_____ drying the dishes soon.

2. She likes to _____ in the water at the pool.

3. There's a lot of _____ in that bin. Can you empty it?

4. I _____ I could fly in real life like I can in my dreams.

5. You can't pull the door. You must _____ it.

6. I like to _____ our cat's fur.

7. He uses his boat to go deep-sea _____.

8. If you pay in _____, you can get a discount.

INITIAL DIGRAPH: *ch*

The digraph *ch* can stand for the sound /ch/, as in *chair*. The digraph *ch* often appears at the beginning of a word.

A. Look at the pictures. Write the letters to complete the words. Then read the words out aloud.

__ __ ick

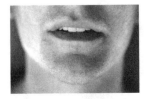

__ __ in

__ __ ess

B. Read the following words out loud. Then write a rhyming word for each that begins with *ch*.

1. less	*chess*	**6.** mild	_____
2. please	_____	**7.** hop	_____
3. win	_____	**8.** stick	_____
4. walk	_____	**9.** meat	_____
5. heap	_____	**10.** strange	_____

C. Complete each sentence with a word from the box below. Then read the sentences out loud.

chain   change   chase   check   chess   chest   chick   chose

1. I _____*chose*_____ the best dog in the pet shop.

2. I have a cold in my head and my _____.

3. My dog likes to _____ his tail when he plays.

4. My clothes were dirty, so I had to _____ them.

5. I like to play _____ with my grandpa.

6. The little yellow _____ is so cute.

7. She has a gold _____ around her neck.

8. I paid for my swimming class with a _____.

FINAL DIGRAPH: *ch*; LETTERS: *tch*

The digraph *ch* can stand for the sound /ch/, as in *each*. The /ch/ sound is often represented by the letters *tch*, as in *catch*. The digraph *ch* and the letters *tch* often appear at the end of words.

A. Look at the pictures. Circle the letters that stand for the sound /ch/. Then read the words out loud.

inch

match

beach

B. Complete each sentence with a word from the box below. Then read the sentences out loud.

beach   hatches   lunch   peach   watch

1. A sweet, fuzzy, yellow fruit is called a _____*peach*_____ .

2. The meal you eat in the afternoon is _____.

3. You can tell what time it is with a _____.

4. You can go to the _____ to swim and get a suntan.

5. A baby chick _____ out of an egg.

C. Correct the underlined word in each sentence if necessary. Then read the sentences out loud.

1. Let's have rice and beans for <u>luntch</u>.   *lunch*

2. I am having a ham <u>sandwich</u> with chips.

3. Can you <u>reach</u> up to the top shelf?

4. Would you like blueberry, apple, or <u>peatch</u> pie?

5. We can <u>wach</u> TV tonight.

6. One <u>intch</u> is equal to about two and a half centimeters.

Name _____ Date _____

INITIAL DIGRAPH: *wh*

The digraph *wh* can stand for the sound /hw/, as in *wheel*. The digraph *wh* appears only at the beginning of a word.

A. Look at the pictures. Circle the letters that stand for the /hw/ sound. Then read the words out loud.

wheel

whale

whisk

B. Complete each sentence with a word from the box below. Then read the sentences out loud.

wheat   when   where   which   white   why

1. _____*When*_____ Dad bakes a cake, our whole home smells good.

2. That loaf is made from whole _____ flour.

3. _____ don't you at least try the fish?

4. _____ did I leave my coat? I can't find it.

5. _____ one of you broke the window?

6. The _____ sweater is mine. The blue one is yours.

C. Read the clues. Complete the puzzle with words from the box. Then read the words out loud.

Across
1. a type of flour
2. not black
3. pronoun for a place

Down
1. a long cry
2. a bike has two of these
3. pronoun for a person

| wheat |
| wheels |
| where |
| whine |
| white |
| who |

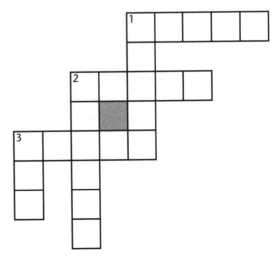

To compare two things, add *-er* to an adjective that ends with two or more consonants. If the adjective ends in a *y,* change the *y* to an *i* before adding *-er.* Notice the use of the word *than* in the examples below.

> (bright) Day is **brighter** than night.
> (shiny) My black boots are **shinier** than my blue ones.

To compare two or more things, add *-est* to an adjective that ends with two or more consonants. If the adjective ends in a *y,* change the *y* to an *i* before adding *-est.* Notice the use of the word *the* in the examples below.

> (old) There are three of us. The **oldest** is 18.
> (pretty) The yellow dress is the **prettiest**.

A. Complete each sentence by adding *-er* or *-est* to the word in parentheses. Then read the sentences out loud.

1. On our trip, we stayed at the _____*fanciest*_____ places we could. (fancy)

2. The train will be much _____ than the bus. (fast)

3. Last night, I slept on the _____ bed yet. (soft)

4. Too bad we came here on the _____ week of the year. (rainy)

5. This trip seemed _____ than the last one. (long)

B. Correct the spelling of the underlined words in the following paragraph. If the word is correct, put a check mark above it. Then read the passage out loud.

Jill's wedding was last Sunday. It was the <u>happyest</u> day of her life. Jill's veil was <u>longest</u>
            1.   2.

than Betty's veil was. Betty's dress was <u>frillyer</u> than Jill's. Jill got a <u>highyer</u> stack of gifts,
                                       3.   4.

but Betty's cake was <u>tastyest</u>. Jill's groom, Rick, is the <u>funnier</u> man I've ever met. It was the
                             5.   6.

<u>grander</u> wedding I have ever been to.
   7.

HIGH FREQUENCY WORDS: Set 9

A. You will see these ten words in many books. Read the words out loud.

| before draw eight every never only pretty seven some work |

B. Read the following passage out loud. Circle the high frequency words.

I love to draw. In fact, I never want to stop drawing. I began drawing when I was five years old. I have seven or eight sketch pads right now. Some of my drawings are pretty good. I mostly just draw what I see. Before I started high school I could only draw trees and buildings, but now I can draw everything. I take drawing classes every Tuesday to help me get even better.

When I get older and go to work, I want drawing to be my job. If I get rich, my sketch pads will cost a lot of money. I put a lot of work into them.

C. Read the passage again. Answer the following questions.

1. How many sketch pads does the writer have?

_____

2. When does the writer take drawing classes?

_____

A. Read the following passage out loud.

My Team

I like playing with my team. I like feeling the hot sun on my face when I stand on the soft grass. I like the smell of a mitt and the feel of a bat. I would run the bases and catch fly balls all day long if they'd let me. I can hit long home runs and help my team win.

My team is named the Mighty Crows. We play after school and on Sundays. Our moms and dads like to see us play. When I am in the field, I don't miss a thing. I keep my eye on the ball, and it lands in my mitt.

We've got a strict coach, Ben. He makes us stretch. He makes us run. He makes us do laps until our legs shake. It isn't so bad; we laugh and have fun, too. Thanks to Coach Ben's training, we're fast and strong. The Mighty Crows are just about the only team to beat. GO TEAM!

B. Read the passage again. Answer the following questions.

1. What game does the writer play?

   _____

2. What is the name of the team?

   _____

 Read the passage to a family member or a friend. Does he or she play a team sport sport? Discuss sports you both like to play.

CHAPTER 4 REVIEW

A. Complete each sentence with a word from the box below. Then read the sentences out loud.

| chess | problem | sandwiches | seven | thanks | that | then | think | when | work |

1. _____*When*_____ do you want to come to my place?

2. I can be there by _____ o'clock.

3. My mom gets home from _____ at six.

4. Do you _____ she could pick me up on her way?

5. I'll ask her, but I'm sure _____ will be fine.

6. _____ can she give me a ride home around nine?

7. I'm sure that won't be a _____.

8. _____ a lot.

9. That's okay. Do you want to play a game of _____ tonight?

10. Sure. I'll bring some _____ to snack on.

B. Correct the underlined words in the following paragraph. Then read the paragraph out loud.

It's been raining all week. Today is the <u>rainier</u> day this week. The grass is <u>greenest</u> than
                                      1.   2.

last week. Things look <u>cleanest</u> and <u>brightest</u>. But not Buddy, our dog. He played in the
                               3.   4.

<u>deeper</u> mud hole that he could find. He's the <u>muddyest</u> dog on the block but he's <u>happyest</u>
5.   6.   7.

when he's muddy.

C. Complete each sentence with a contraction using the word or words in parentheses. Then read the sentences out loud.

1. I (cannot) _____*can't*_____ see very well.

2. I hope I (do not) _____ need glasses.

3. I (would not) _____ mind getting contact lenses.

4. Contact lenses (are not) _____ so bad.

5. Steve has contact lenses. He (does not) _____ like them.

6. He says they (do not) _____ feel right.

7. (He is) _____ going to get glasses instead.

8. Maybe (I will) _____ just get glasses too.

9. (I would) _____ get cool black frames.

10. Then (we would) _____ both have glasses.

D. Read the clues. Answer with words from the box. Then read the answers out loud.

| chick   chilly   shiny   shop   thief |

1. cold one who wins   _____*chilly*_____ champ

2. bright home for a crab   _____ shell

3. a hen's fat offspring   chubby _____

4. skinny man who steals   thin _____

5. place to buy bed linens   sheet _____

CHAPTER 5   **MORE VOWEL PATTERNS AND COMPLEX CONSONANTS**

R-controlled /är/: *ar* 108

The /ô/ Sound: *a, aw, au* 109

R-controlled /ôr/: *or, ore, our, ar* 110

R-controlled /ûr/: *er, ir, ur, or, ear* 111

Schwa /ər/: *er* 112

High Frequency Words: Set 10 113

Reading Practice: Passage 10 114

R-controlled /âr/: *are, air* 115

Word Analysis: CVrC, CVrCe Syllables 116

Initial and Final /f/: *ph* 117

Initial /r/: *wr* 118

Initial /n/: *kn* 119

Initial and Final /n/: *gn* 120

Final *mb* and *bt*: Silent *b* 121

High Frequency Words: Set 11 122

Reading Practice: Passage 11 123

Chapter 5 Review 124

R-CONTROLLED /är/: ar

The sound /är/ is often an *r*-controlled vowel sound. Usually, when an *a* is followed by an *r*, /är/ sounds like the *ar* in *car*.

A. Look at the pictures. Write the letters to complete the words. Then read the words out loud.

c __ __ __   __ t __ __   __ __ t

B. Complete the following words with the *r*-controlled /är/ sound. Then read the words out loud.

1. sp__*ar*__k   7. f_____m

2. _____m   8. c_____t

3. f_____   9. st_____t

4. h_____d   10. m_____k

5. sm_____t   11. sc_____

6. h_____p   12. c_____

C. Complete each sentence with a word from the box below. Then read the sentences out loud.

barn   March   park   scarf   starts

1. The new movie _____*starts*_____ showing this Friday.

2. You can find sheep and goats in the big red _____.

3. We camped in our tent at a state _____.

4. The _____ on his neck has red stars.

5. The month of _____ can be cold or mild.

Name _____ Date _____

The /ô/ Sound: *a, aw, au*

The /ô/ sound can be spelled:

- *aw,* as in *saw*
- *a,* as in *salt*
- *au,* as in *haunt*

A. Look at the pictures. Write the letters to complete the words. Then read the words out loud.

__ __ w

__ __ l __

B. Complete each sentence with a word from the box below. Then read the sentences out loud.

all ball launch mall saw tall

1. I like to play _____ *ball* _____ with the kids on the block.

2. Our best teammate is Walt. He's very _____.

3. The kids on the block like Walt a lot and they _____ want to be on his team.

4. After school we spend time at the _____.

5. You can _____ your boat from this dock.

6. We _____ Ken play the part of Puck in the school play.

C. Write sentences using the words in the box below. Then read the sentences out loud.

ball	bawled	claws	crawled	fall	haul	jaw
law	paws	salt	saw	small	vault	wall

1. _The claws in that cat's paws are sharp._____

2. _____

3. _____

4. _____

Chapter 5 • *R-*controlled Vowels

R-CONTROLLED /ôr/: *or, ore, our, ar*

The sound /ôr/ is often an *r*-controlled sound. The sound /ôr/ can be spelled:

- *or,* as in *for*
- *ore,* as in *more*
- *our,* as in *pour*
- *ar,* as in *war*

A. Look at the pictures. Write the letters to complete the words. Then read the words out loud.

c __ __ n

st __ __ __

__ __ __ r

B. Read the following words out loud. Draw lines to connect the words that rhyme.

1. warm   wart

2. for   torch

3. court   chores

4. mourn   born

5. porch   storm

6. wars   more

C. Complete each sentence with a word from the box below. Then read the sentences out loud.

| fork   more   porch   pour   short |

1. Will you please _____*pour*_____ me some milk?

2. I like high heels because I am _____.

3. Our house has a big _____. We enjoy sitting there in the evenings.

4. I want to have one _____ glass of milk.

5. The baby is learning to eat with a _____.

Name _____ Date _____

R-CONTROLLED /ûr/: er, ir, ur, or, ear

The sound /ûr/ is often an *r*-controlled vowel sound. The sound /ûr/ can be spelled:

- *er,* as in *fern*
- *ir,* as in *bird*
- *ur,* as in *turn*
- *or,* as in *world*
- *ear,* as in *learn*

A. Look at the pictures. Write the letters to complete the words. Then read the words out loud.

f __ __ n   w __ __ __ __   b __ __ __

B. Complete each sentence with a word from the box below. Then read the sentences out loud.

burn Earth her learn skirt turn work worth

1. She wore a black and green _____*skirt*_____ with a green top.

2. You can _____ to play the flute if you want to.

3. A tadpole will _____ into a frog.

4. The _____ is the third planet from the Sun.

5. She will walk _____ brother home from school.

6. This artwork is _____ a lot of money.

7. Please turn the flame down so you won't _____ the oatmeal.

8. She wants to _____ as a doctor when she finishes college.

C. Read the rhyme out loud. Then underline the words that contain the /ûr/ sound.

She <u>twirls</u> and she <u>turns</u> as light as you please,

The quick, perky girl on the flying trapeze.

She leaps from her perch and we see her fly,

As free of the world as a bird in the sky.

Schwa /ər/: er

The schwa sound is common in English. All five vowels (a, e, i, o, u) can stand for the schwa sound. The letters er often stand for the schwa sound.

A. Look at the pictures. Write the letters to complete the words. Then read the words out loud.

d __ __ c __ __

b __ __ t __ __

B. Complete each sentence with a word from the box below. Then read the sentences out loud.

> bother   number   runner   under

1. She is the fastest _____ on the track and field team.

2. Pick a _____ from one to ten.

3. The cat is sleeping _____ the table.

4. Please don't _____ me while I study.

C. Read the clues. Complete the puzzle with words from the box. Then read the words out loud.

> grower   gutter   letter   litter   never   over   River   sitter

Across

1. a farmer is a crop _____
4. to drop trash in a park
5. not ever
6. a pet _____ cares for cats and dogs

Down

1. a drain around the roof
2. not under, but _____
3. the Mississippi _____
4. a vowel or a consonant

HIGH FREQUENCY WORDS: Set 10

A. You will see these ten words in many books. Read the words out loud.

| carry   group   live   many   out   over   people   pull   together   warm |

B. Read the following passage. Circle the high frequency words.

Henry and I camped out together over the weekend. For two days, we got to live in a tent. Saturday morning we had to carry a lot of logs and sticks over to our camp so we could burn them and stay warm. There weren't many people camping, but there was a nice group in the campsite to our left.

We stayed warm all night in our sleeping bags. I had to pull on my thick socks to keep warm on Sunday morning because it was cool out. On Sunday afternoon, we went rafting with the group of people in the next campsite. We had to carry their raft up the river. Then we rode down over the rapids together. At the end of the ride, we had to work hard to pull the raft out of the river. Henry and I made many new pals. We all plan to get together as a group again one day soon. Still, it was a little sad to pull up our tent stakes and go home.

C. Read the passage again. Answer the following questions.

1. Where did the writer and his friend live for two days?

_____

2. What did they do on Sunday afternoon?

_____

A. Read the following passage out loud.

Brave Rich

Rich jumps out of a plane and floats down. His goal: to reach that wildfire. He wants to get inches away. Is Rich nuts? No, he's a smokejumper. Rich is brave. He is a highly trained firefighter. Rich's job is to put out wildfires so they can't catch onto trees and get too big to beat back.

Rich works with a team. Their team goes to fires that most firefighters can't get to. They get to the fires quickly by plane. When a fire alarm goes off, Rich and his team run to the plane and put on their packs. The plane flies over trees. Rich and his team see the fire. It's time for Rich and his team to jump out and fight a big fire. Trees, plants, animals, and a lot of wildlife need Rich to help them stay safe.

B. Read the passage again. Answer the following questions.

1. What does Rich jump out of?

   _____

2. What is Rich's job?

   _____

 Read the passage to a family member or a friend. Discuss Rich's dangerous job. Do you think he is brave? Why or why not?

Name _____ Date _____

The /âr/ sound is often an *r*-controlled vowel sound. The /âr/ sound is usually spelled *are* and *air*.

A. Look at the pictures. Write the letters to complete the words. Then read the words out loud.

ch __ __ __   squ __ __ __   st __ __ __

B. Complete each set of sentences with a pair of words from the box below. Then read the sentences out loud.

fair/fare   hare/hair   pare/pair   stare/stair

1 a. Would you like to go to the arts and crafts _____*fair*_____ with me?

   b. The _____*fare*_____ will be higher in November because of Thanksgiving.

2 a. I own one _____ of boots.

   b. You can _____ ginger with the sharp side of a spoon.

3 a. Please don't _____ at people. It's rude.

   b. Easy does it. Just take one _____ at a time to reach the top.

4 a. The _____ is a fast rabbit, but he doesn't finish the race first.

   b. I don't want the wind to mess up my _____.

C. Read the clues. Write the correct rhyming words from the box.

air   bare   chair   fair   fare   hair   square   stair

1. seat with nothing in it   _____*bare*_____   _____*chair*_____

2. price of a plane ticket   _____   _____

3. a step with equal sides   _____   _____

4. a blond girl has this   _____   _____

WORD ANALYSIS: CVrC, CVrCe Syllables

Many words with *r*-controlled vowel sounds have the CVrC pattern, such as *bird, turn,* and *corn*. Another common pattern having *r*-controlled vowel sounds is CVrCe. In this pattern, the *e* is silent. For example, *scarce* has the same *r*-controlled vowel sound as *pair*; *horse* has the same vowel sound as *cord*.

A. Complete each sentence with a word from the box below. Then read the sentences out loud.

burn first horse large nurse served urge

1. The waiter _____*served*_____ us our meal.

2. The _____ one to the finish line wins the race.

3. If you don't have sunscreen, stay in the shade or you may _____.

4. Speak with the _____ if you are not feeling well.

5. It might be fun to ride a _____, but not a goat.

6. Pick up some _____ eggs at the store, not jumbo and not small.

7. I would _____ you to invest some time in homework each day.

B. Read the following words out loud. Find and circle the words.

carve
charge
murky
nurse
serve
shore
verse
wares

c	i	r	v	n	w	g	m
h	o	i	e	u	a	a	u
a	r	n	r	r	r	d	r
r	a	e	s	s	e	r	k
g	d	v	e	e	s	e	y
e	u	r	r	s	r	n	m
c	a	r	v	e	t	v	e
k	n	c	s	h	o	r	e

Name _____ Date _____

INITIAL and FINAL /f/: *ph*

The /f/ sound can be spelled with the digraph *ph*. The digraph *ph* can appear at the beginning of a word, such as *phone*, or at the end of a word or a syllable, such as *telegraph*.

A. Look at the pictures. Write the letters to complete the words. Then read the words out loud.

_ _ _ ne   _ _ ot _   gra _ _

B. Complete the following words with the digraph /ph/. Read the words out loud.

1. __*ph*__ase

2. _____obic

3. em_____atic

4. _____yllo

5. _____ysics

6. sta_____

7. _____ony

8. _____os_____ate

9. _____oton

10. _____onics

C. Complete each sentence with a word from the box below. Then read the sentences out loud.

> graph   phone   phonics   photo   photon   physics

1. A _____*photon*_____ is much, much smaller than the size of this dot.

2. The study of matter and energy is _____.

3. Call me later on my cell _____.

4. Draw a bar _____ to show how the costs have changed.

5. We have a _____ of them on their wedding day.

6. Studying _____ is a great way to learn a language.

The /r/ sound can be spelled with the letters *wr*, as in *write*. When the letters *wr* stand for the sound /r/, *wr* appears at the beginning of the word. The *w* is silent.

A. Look at the pictures. Write the letters to complete the words. Then read the words out loud.

__ __ ench   __ __ ist   __ __ eath

B. Complete each sentence with a word from the box below. Then read the sentences out loud.

wrap   wreck   wrench   write

1. I will _____ you a letter when you go away.

2. I will _____ the gift in red paper for her birthday.

3. Two cars got in a _____ down the street, but no one was hurt.

4. Dad used a _____ to fix our sink.

C. Read the following words out loud. Find and circle the word.

wrap
wreck
wring
wrist
write
wrong
wrote

i	w	d	e	r	c	w
w	r	i	t	e	o	r
r	i	e	d	u	e	i
o	n	l	c	t	l	s
n	g	o	o	t	a	t
g	o	r	l	a	r	n
e	w	r	e	c	k	h
w	r	a	p	d	a	d

Name _____ Date _____

INITIAL /n/: *kn*

The /n/ sound can be spelled with the letters *kn*, as in *know*. When the letters *kn* stand for the /n/ sound, *kn* appears at the beginning of the word. The *k* is silent.

A. Look at the pictures. Write the letters to complete the words. Then read the words out loud.

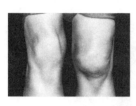      

__ __ ee   __ __ ife   __ __ ot

B. Complete each sentence with a word from the box below. Then read the sentences out loud.

knee   kneel   knit   knob   knock   knot   know

1. Pull the _____*knob*_____ to open the dresser.

2. Will you please _____ me a warm, pretty scarf?

3. If you _____ harder, she might let you in.

4. I need to bend my _____ to do this exercise.

5. If you tie a _____ in the rope, it will help you hold on.

6. Do you _____ much about physics?

7. You might have to _____ down to talk to a small child.

C. Read the clues. Answer with a word that begins with *kn*. Then put together the underlined letters to answer the last clue.

1. where your leg bends

k	n	e	e

2. to understand is to _____ how

3. to make a scarf with yarn

4. *know* in the past form

5. to tie a rope, you make a

Chapter 5 • *R*-controlled Vowels

INITIAL and FINAL /n/: *gn*

The /n/ sound can be spelled with the letters *gn*, as in *designer*. The letters *gn* can appear at the beginning or end of a word or syllable, as in *gnaw*. The *g* is silent.

A. Look at the pictures. Write the letters to complete the words. Then read the words out loud.

__ __ ome

si __ __

__ __ u

B. Complete each sentence with a word from the box below. Then read the sentences out loud.

campaign   gnarly   gnash   gnat   gnaw   sign

1. The bumps on that tree's roots make it _____*gnarly*_____.

2. Rodney will start his _____ six weeks before we vote.

3. A _____ is a small insect.

4. Look both ways after you stop at a stop _____.

5. Big cats such as tigers hunt fresh meat and _____ on bones.

6. A monster might _____ its teeth to scare us.

C. Complete the following words with *n*, *kn*, or *gn*. Then read the words out loud.

1. __*kn*__ife

2. _____ight

3. _____u

4. _____aw

5. _____ick_____ack

6. _____eecap

7. _____ot

8. _____at

9. si_____

10. _____ash

11. _____est

12. _____ome

Chapter 5 • *R*-controlled Vowels

Name _____ Date _____

FINAL *mb* and *bt:* Silent *b*

Sometimes two letters at the end of a word can stand for one sound.

- The letters *mb* at the end of a word stand for the /m/ sound. The *b* is silent.
- The letters *bt* at the end of a word stand for the /t/ sound. The *b* is silent.

A. Look at the pictures. Write the letters to complete the words. Then read the words out loud.

co __ __

th __ __ __

de __ t

B. Complete each sentence with a word from the box below. Then read the sentences out loud.

| climb   comb   crumb   debt   lamb |

1. I ate my whole sandwich. Not a _____*crumb*_____ is left.

2. I owe Mom ten dollars. I will pay my _____ next week.

3. I always _____ my hair before going to school.

4. I will try to _____ up that hill.

5. A baby sheep is called a _____.

C. Read the clues. Complete the puzzle with words from the box. Then read the words out loud.

| climb   crumb   debt   dumb   lamb   limb |

Across

2. arm or leg; also part of a tree

3. to go up

4. not smart

Down

1. money you owe

2. baby sheep

3. bit of cake or cookie

Chapter 5 • *R*-controlled Vowels

A. You will see these ten words in many books. Read the words out loud.

answer   any   common   decision   fear   friend   hear   listen   questions   summary

B. Read the following passage. Circle the high frequency words.

Speaking in public is a common fear, I hear. The fear can grab you at any time. Well, it grabbed me. I had to give a summary of a film. I asked myself: Will people listen? What if I can't answer any of their questions? I made a decision. I could not do this.

"What's up?" my friend Maddie asked me, and I told her.

"We have something in common," she said. "You can do that summary. I'll listen to your speech. Speak up so I can hear you."

I gave the summary. Maddie listened. I answered her questions. Everything was fine. Then I made a new decision. I could do this speech.

C. Read the passage again. Answer the following questions.

1. According to the writer, what is a common fear?

_____

2. What did the writer do to help her with this fear?

_____

Chapter 5   •   *R*-controlled Vowels

READING PRACTICE: Passage 11

A. Read the passage out loud.

Meet Fern Clark

There are three kids in the Clark family. The first kid is Fern. Fern is fifteen, and she likes to work on cars. Her dad's friend gave her an old junky car, and Fern is trying to fix it up. She uses her tool set to work on the engine, and she tries to get it purring again. She tries many things but hasn't been able to get it going. She won't give up. Fern will have her license to drive when she is sixteen, and she wants to pull it together by then.

Fern will drive to school. She will drive her mom to work. She will take the little Clarks, Sam and Dan, to the park. Fern has big plans for her car. That is why Fern will not give up until that car is purring like a kitten.

B. Read the passage again. Answer the following questions.

1. Who is the oldest kid in the Clark family?

_____

2. What is Fern trying to fix up?

_____

Copyright © by Pearson Education, Inc.

Home-School Connection Read the passage to a family member or a friend. Discuss Fern's goal of fixing up her car. Does that person have a goal? Do you?

A. Complete each sentence with a word from the box below. Then read the sentences out loud.

bark	bars	bird	birthday	curly	far	first	fur	shelter	short

1. At last, Dad said I could have a dog. This is my _____*first*_____ dog!

2. We visited a _____ to find him.

3. It is not very _____ from our home.

4. The pretty blue _____ flies to my window every morning.

5. I saw one with a _____ tail, like a pig's.

6. I saw a tall dog and a _____ dog.

7. Our dogs _____ when they see strangers.

8. I slipped my hand between the _____ of his pen.

9. The polar bear had soft, white _____.

10. This dog was the best _____ gift.

B. Correct the spelling of the underlined words. If the word is correct, put a check mark above it. Then read the conversation out loud.

Brad: Mom! Don't panic, but I just cut my <u>fingur</u> with a <u>nife</u>. Please get the <u>fone</u> and call
1.   2.   3.

911. My whole arm feels <u>num</u>.
4.

Mom: Listen, that cut may <u>hert</u>, but I can take care of you here. I have a first-aid kit in my
5.

<u>purs</u>. I will clean and <u>rap</u> your finger, and if it show <u>sines</u> of getting worse, we'll call
6.   7.   8.

a <u>nerse</u>.
9.

CHAPTER 5 REVIEW (continued)

C. Circle the correct word to complete each sentence. Then read the sentences out loud.

1. I will (**wrap**/rap) her gift in red paper.

2. Turn left after the next stop (sighing/sign).

3. Turn your (phase/face) this way, and I'll take your photo.

4. Tell her to (right/write) me a long letter.

5. I got two (new/gnu) pairs of pants yesterday.

6. I (new/knew) I would be late if I stopped at the mall.

7. I will (come/comb) my hair before I go downstairs.

8. Do you (need/knead) help with your homework?

9. (Wring/Ring) that rag until it is just about dry, then hang it up.

10. I am (knot/not) going to the party.

D. Read the clues. Complete the puzzle with words from the box. Then read the words out loud.

| dirty   girl   party   pork   skirt   third |

Across

1. pig meat
2. not clean
3. number three in line

Down

1. a fun event
4. item of clothing
5. a sister is one

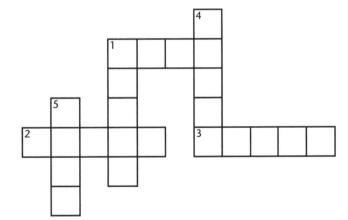

CHAPTER 6   **VOWEL TEAMS**

Vowel Team: *oi* 128

Vowel Team: *oy* 129

Vowel Team: *ou* 130

Vowel Team: *ow* 131

Vowel Teams: *ew, ui, ou, ue, oe* 132

Vowel Teams: *oo, ou;* Vowel: *u* 133

Vowel Teams: *ei, ea, ey* 134

Schwa /əl/: *le* 135

Schwa /ə/: *a* 136

Schwa /ə/: *e, i* 137

Schwa /ə/: *o, u* 138

High Frequency Words: Set 12 139

Reading Practice: Passage 12 140

Word Analysis: Open Syllables: Long *a* 141

Word Analysis: Open Syllables: Long *e* 142

Word Analysis: Open Syllables: Long *i* 143

Word Analysis: Open Syllables: Long *o* 144

Word Analysis: Open Syllables: Long *u* 145

Word Analysis: Vowel Team: Review 146

Word Analysis: Cle Syllables 147

High Frequency Words: Set 13 148

Reading Practice: Passage 13 149

Chapter 6 Review 150

VOWEL TEAM: *oi*

A vowel team is when two vowels appear together and have one sound. The vowel team *oi* often sounds like /oi/, as in *boil*.

A. Look at the pictures. Write the letters to complete the words. Then read the words out loud.

c __ __ ns

__ __ l

B. Complete each sentence with a word from the box below. Then read the sentences out loud.

boil   broil   foil   join   moist   oil

1. Will you _____*join*_____ us for a picnic?

2. The hot dogs are wrapped in aluminum _____.

3. Brush the meat with a little olive _____.

4. That will keep it _____, not dry.

5. We can _____ corn on the cob in that pot.

6. Let's put the meat on the fire to _____.

C. Read the clues. Fill in the spaces with words that have the /oi/ sound spelled *oi*. Then read the words out loud.

1. another name for dirt

s			

2. to go bad

s	p			l

3. aluminum _____

f			

4. a tip of a pencil

p				

Name _____ Date _____

VOWEL TEAM: *oy*

The vowel team *oy* often sounds like /oi/, as in *boy*.

A. Look at the pictures. Write the letters to complete the words. Then read the words out loud.

b __ __

t __ __ s

B. Complete each sentence with a word from the box below. Then read the sentences out loud.

boy   enjoy   joy   toy

1. This _____ store sells dolls, games, and more.

2. Do you _____ meeting new people?

3. That little _____ wants a toy car for his birthday.

4. A feeling of _____ rose up in all of us when we heard the song.

C. Read the clues. Complete the puzzle with words form the word box. Then read the words out loud.

boy   destroy   employ   enjoy   joy   toys

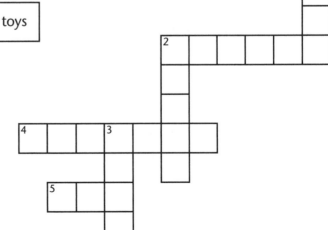

Across

2. to give a job to

4. to wreck

5. not a girl

Down

1. happiness

2. to like

3. dolls, blocks, video games

Chapter 6 • Vowel Teams

VOWEL TEAM: *ou*

The vowel team *ou* often sounds like /ou/, as in *out*.

A. Look at the pictures. Read the following words with /ou/ out loud. Then circle the letters that stand for the /ou/ sound.

clouds

house

B. Read the pairs of words out loud. Circle the word that has the /ou/ sound.

1. grow   (round)   **4.** toy   count   **7.** outline   spoil

2. bounty   bunny   **5.** loud   lose   **8.** sun   out

3. trip   trout   **6.** proud   post   **9.** prove   counter

C. Complete each sentence with a word from the box below. Then read the sentences aloud.

| count   county   foul   found   ground   mouth   outside   shout |

1. What _____*country*_____ is your city in?

2. I lost my wallet, but my mother _____ it.

3. The dentist told me to open my _____ wide.

4. It was such a nice day that I went _____ to hang out.

5. I can _____ to one hundred in French!

6. You don't have to _____. I can hear you just fine.

7. I dropped my lunch on the _____, so I decided not to eat it.

8. The baseball player hit a _____ ball into the stands.

Name _____ Date _____

The vowel team *ow* often sounds like /ou/, as in *now*.

A. Look at the pictures. Write the letters to complete the words. Then read the words out loud.

c __ __   cr __ __ n   __ __ l

B. Read the following words out loud. Draw lines to connect words that rhyme. Then circle the words that have the /ou/ sound spelled with *ow*.

1. crowned	doe
2. power	foul
3. more	own
4. down	crown
5. known	foal
6. grow	round
7. bowl	flour
8. growl	pour

C. Complete each sentence with a word from the box below. Then read the sentences out loud.

bow brown clown cowboy down power

1. The _____*cowboy*_____ rides his horse as he works on the ranch.

2. His horse has a dark _____ coat.

3. The horse is strong and has a lot of _____.

4. He tips his hat _____ over his face for shade.

5. At the rodeo, there is a _____ that makes people smile and laugh.

6. When the clown is finished he will take a _____.

VOWEL TEAMS: *ew, ui, ou, ue, oe*

The vowel teams *ew, ui, ou, ue* and *oe* often have the sound /o͞o/, as in *knew*.

A. Look at the pictures. Read the words out loud. Then circle the letters that stand for the /o͞o/ sound.

news   suit   soup   glue

B. Read the following words out loud. Cross out the word in each group that does not have the /o͞o/ sound.

1. dew	shoe	does	due	grew
2. fruit	true	ground	noon	group
3. shoot	cloud	soup	soon	clue
4. food	loop	flew	how	blue
5. new	spoon	tooth	loud	you

C. Complete each sentence with a word from the box below. Then read the sentences out loud.

> broom   flute   fruit   juice   soup   true   who

1. We like to make _____*juice*_____ from the grapes in our yard.

2. _____ is a healthful snack.

3. We cleaned up the broken glass with a _____.

4. Do you know if it's _____ that June moved?

5. _____ told you that?

6. My brother plays the _____ in the school band.

7. We are having vegetable _____ for dinner.

VOWEL TEAMS: *oo, ou;* VOWEL: *u*

The vowel teams *oo, ou,* and the vowel *u* often have the sound /ŏŏ/, as in *book.*

A. Look at the pictures. Read the following words out loud. Then circle the letters that stand for the /ŏŏ/ sound.

      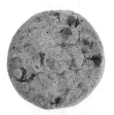

book   **bull**   **cookie**

B. Complete each sentence with a word from the box below. Then read the sentences out loud.

> bush   cook   could   foot   look   should

1. Can you zoom in with that lens so we can get a closer _____*look*_____?

2. My _____ is too big to fit in that shoe.

3. I'm hungry. I hope Mom is going to _____.

4. We pick a lot of berries from the _____ in our backyard.

5. _____ you open the door for me, please?

6. We _____ leave early if we want to get good seats.

C. Read the clues. Fill in the spaces with words that contain /ŏŏ/ spelled *oo.* Then read the words out loud.

1. he works at a stove | c | | | |

2. past tense of shake | s | | | | k |

3. you read this | b | | | |

4. opposite of push | | | l | l |

5. to see | l | | | |

6. past tense of will | w | | | | d |

VOWEL TEAMS: *ei, ea, ey*

The vowel teams *ei, ea,* and *ey* often have the sound /ā/, as in *they*. When *gh* follows *ei,* the *gh* is silent, as in *weigh.*

A. Look at the pictures. Read the following words out loud. Then circle the letters that stand for the /ā/ sound.

| steak | veil | neighbor |

B. Read the pairs of words out loud. Circle the word that has the /ā/ sound.

1. sleep   vein
2. break   fat
3. reign   lie
4. right   neighbor
5. they   them
6. hey   high
7. bean   sleigh
8. freight   fright
9. bat   eight
10. blew   grey
11. their   great
12. weigh   vine

C. Complete each sentence with a word pair from the box below. Then read the sentences out loud.

> break/brake   eight/ate   great/grate   hey/hay   pray/prey   weigh/way

1. I _____*ate*_____ _____*eight*_____ grapes and three cookies.

2. One _____ to _____ a cat is to hold it and stand on a scale.

3. It would be _____ if you could _____ the cheese for our supper.

4. Step on the _____, or you will hit the bike and _____ it.

5. _____! Let's go for a _____ ride at the Miller's farm this fall.

6. I _____ the tiger doesn't make me its _____.

Name _____ Date _____

Schwa /əl/: *le*

Usually when *-le* is at the end of a word and has a consonant before it, the consonant + *-le* forms the last syllable. The sound between the consonant and *-le* is called a schwa.

A. Look at the pictures. Read the following words out loud. Then circle the schwa sound.

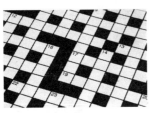
puzzle

waffle

bumble bee

B. Read each pair of words out loud. Circle the word that has the /ə/ sound.

1. possible	positive	**6.** measles	mumps
2. monkey	uncle	**7.** sizzle	fresh
3. battle	battery	**8.** maybe	mumble
4. tremble	tremendous	**9.** waffle	pancake
5. violin	fiddle	**10.** standing	stumble

C. Complete each sentence with a word or phrase from the box below. Then read the sentences out loud.

> apple bottle bumble bee middle puzzle settle

1. Grades six to eight are _____*middle*_____ school.

2. A black and yellow _____ landed on the flower.

3. I have an _____ and a sandwich for my lunch today.

4. I had a _____ of orange juice with my lunch.

5. This _____ is too hard for me to figure out.

6. Do your best, and don't _____ for less.

Schwa /ə/: *a*

When the letter *a* is in an unstressed syllable, the sound of the *a* can be weakened and become a schwa sound.

A. Look at the pictures. Read the following words out loud. Then circle the letters that stand for the /ə/ sound.

alarm

banana   lizard

B. Complete each sentence with a word from the box below. Then read the sentences out loud.

afraid   ago   alone   around   asleep   awhile   medical

1. A while _____*ago*_____, I found three puppies.

2. The mother dog had left them _____.

3. When I found them, they were not awake, they were _____.

4. They were _____ of me at first, but then they began to like me.

5. They needed _____ help from a vet.

6. In _____, the puppies got better.

7. They run _____ all day chewing on my stuff.

C. Read the clues. Unscramble the letters. Each answer contains /ə/ spelled *a*. Write the word on the line. Then read the words out loud.

1. someone from America   canerAmic   _____

2. not here   aayw   _____

3. not asleep   kewaa   _____

4. a yellow fruit   aaabnn   _____

5. machine that wakes you   malar   _____

Name _____ Date _____

When the letter *e* or *i* is in an unstressed syllable, the sound of the *e* or *i* can be weakened and become a schwa sound.

A. **Look at the pictures. Read the following words out loud. Then circle the letters that stand for the /ə/ sound.**

weasel   pencil   oven

B. **Read the following words out loud. Underline the vowels that have the /ə/ sound.**

1. buck<u>e</u>t   6. written

2. taken   7. ticket

3. kitten   8. easily

4. happen   9. happily

5. family   10. shaken

C. **Complete each sentence with a word from the box below. Then read the sentences out loud.**

| cousin   garden   oven   pencil   taken   ticket |

1. I am going to visit my aunt and my _____ this weekend.

2. There are red, white, and yellow roses growing in our _____.

3. Please turn off the _____. The cake is done.

4. Will you sharpen this _____ for me?

5. I got a _____ for the concert.

6. I've _____ many exams, but this one was the hardest.

Schwa /ə/: *o, u*

When the letter *o* or *u* is in an unstressed syllable, the sound of the *o* or *u* can be weakened and become a schwa sound.

A. Look at the pictures. Read the following words out loud. Then circle the letters that stand for the /ə/ sound.

container

circus

opossum

B. Read the following words out loud. Underline the vowels that have the /ə/ sound spelled with an *o* or *u*.

1. poison	**6.** edible	**11.** faculty	**16.** aware
2. comma	**7.** doctor	**12.** tomato	**17.** ketchup
3. gallop	**8.** open	**13.** vacuum	**18.** medium
4. phantom	**9.** modern	**14.** biology	
5. sister	**10.** problem	**15.** harden	

C. Complete each sentence with a word from the box below. Then read the sentences out loud.

> Clinton   circus   faculty   poison   second   tomato   venom

1. "B" is the _____*second*_____ letter of the alphabet.

2. The forty-second president of the United States was Bill _____.

3. Some snake bites release _____.

4. Snake venom can _____ you.

5. Lettuce, cucumber, and _____ make a nice salad.

6. All of the teachers at a school are called the _____.

7. We saw elephants, horses, and acrobats at the _____.

HIGH FREQUENCY WORDS: Set 12

A. You will see these ten words in many books. Read the words out loud.

although	character	culture	father	mother
once	sure	thought	through	vocabulary

B. Read the words in passage again. Circle the high frequency words.

Every family has its own culture. Culture means how people act, how they express themselves through art, what their beliefs are, what they do on holidays, and other products of their work and thought. Sure, family culture is a small example compared to the culture of the United States. Still, although it is small, it is significant. Once a mother hangs her child's first artwork on the wall, she has started the family gallery. When a father praises his child's artwork, he is shaping that child's character. Through nicknames and endearments, a family starts its own cultural language with its own vocabulary. Each family member is a character in some story that is sure to be told at the next family gathering. Each family, within a larger culture, has its own one-of-a-kind culture to enjoy.

C. Read the passage again. Answer the following questions.

1. According to the passage, what does *culture* mean?

   _____

2. How can a family start its own cultural language?

   _____

A. Read the following passage out loud.

The Animal Shelter

This summer I am volunteering at the animal shelter near my home. I help dogs get adopted. There are all kinds of dogs there: poodles, huskies, terriers, black and yellow labs, setters, bulldogs, beagles, and more. I play with them and walk them. This makes a dog happy. A happy dog is more likely to find a permanent home.

Sometimes I get attached to a dog. That's what happened with Max, a sweet bulldog. We became instant buddies. Then one day, a mother with two children came in, and they all fell in love with Max. Just like that, they took him home. I was happy for Max but sad for me. It made me think it might be time to adopt a dog of my own. I talked to my mother and father about it, and they said, sure, as long as I take care of it. And, as long as it's just one!

B. Read the passage again. Answer the following questions.

1. What kind of work does the narrator do?

   _____

2. Why might you describe the ending as happy?

   _____

Read the passage to a family member or a friend. Has that person ever adopted a pet from a shelter? Have you? Discuss your opinion about animal shelters.

WORD ANALYSIS: Open Syllables: Long *a*

Every syllable contains a vowel sound. A syllable ending with a vowel sound is called an open syllable. When the open syllable has a long vowel sound, as in *baby*, it is usually stressed.

A. Read the following words out loud. Circle the open syllables.

a/pron   wa/vy   na/vy   vol/ca/no

B. Read the following words out loud. Put a slash between the syllables. Circle the open syllable with the long *a* sound.

1. (pa)/per   4. basis   7. chaos   10. acorn   13. patient

2. labor   5. able   8. famous   11. nasal   14. native

3. cradle   6. razor   9. cable   12. baby   15. gracious

C. Read the clues. Write an open syllable with *a* to complete the words. Then read the words out loud.

1. vegetable used to make french fries   po___*ta*___to

2. something you write on   _____per

3. something you might do for someone else   _____vor

4. another name for a woman   _____dy

5. doesn't work very hard   _____zy

D. Read the following words out loud. Circle the words with the /ā/ sound. Underline the words that have an open syllable with /ā/ spelled *a*.

(table)	fate	fat	statistic	they	bagel	great	lacy	gait
lady	crazy	later	trait	cat	late	pal	pail	chaser
trade	tan	weigh	lay	tray	fable	break	beak	loan
fatal	tidal	maid	gnat	said	traitor	trail	veil	hey

A syllable ending with a vowel sound is called an open syllable. When the open syllable has a long vowel sound, as in *zebra*, it is usually stressed.

A. Read the following words out loud. Circle the open syllables.

e/ven   ze/bra   pre/fix   le/gal

B. Read the following words out loud. Put a slash between the syllables. Circle the open syllable with the long *e* sound.

1. (re)/cent   3. secret   5. Peter   7. equal   9. evil

2. meter   4. female   6. even   8. penal   10. email

C. Read the clues. Unscramble the syllables to find the answer. Then read the answers out loud.

1. woman   malefe   _____female_____

2. royal   aegrl   _____

3. a small part   diltae   _____

4. time for play   cessre   _____

5. striped animal   braze   _____

D. Read the following words out loud. Circle each word with the /ē/ sound. Underline the word that have an open syllable with /ē/ spelled *e*.

(speak)	seen	he	breaks	tea	e-mail	grief	green
team	she	we	they	heat	need	neat	donkey
funny	money	regal	sender	entire	lean	head	item
steam	meets	gate	meat	be	bed	cliff	great

WORD ANALYSIS: Open Syllables: Long *i*

A syllable ending with a vowel sound is called an open syllable. When the open syllable has a long vowel sound, as in *minor*, it is usually stressed.

A. Read the following words out loud. Circle the open syllables.

i/tem   si/lent   Chi/na   spi/der

B. Read the following words out loud. Put a slash between the syllables. Circle the open syllable with the long *i* sound.

1. mi/grate   4. vibrate   7. bible   10. biker   13. diner

2. vital   5. Dinah   8. cider   11. climber   14. wiper

3. final   6. dial   9. client   12. biceps   15. diet

C. Complete each sentence with a word from the box below. Then read the sentences out loud.

| biceps final lilacs rival title virus |

1. Our football _____*rival*_____ is the Mount Holyoke team.

2. I have a stuffy nose. I hope I haven't caught a _____.

3. Please add some _____ into that bunch of flowers.

4. Doing push-ups will strengthen your _____.

5. Our _____ exam is on June fifteenth.

6. What is the _____ of the book you told me to read?

D. Read the following words out loud. Circle the word with the /ī/ sound. Underline the words that have an open syllable with /ī/ spelled *i*.

light	veil	gain	bind	lip	sky	dine	tidal
minor	fin	final	bride	bridal	microphone	physics	cry
sing	line	mitten	mind	triceps	trip	tries	sticks
file	lime	pilot	night	like	cried	fly	idol

A syllable ending with vowel sound is called an open syllable. When the open syllable has a long vowel sound, as in *hotel*, it is usually stressed.

A. Read the following words out loud. Circle the open syllables.

to/tem   mo/ment   o/pen   fo/cus

B. Read the following words out loud. Put a slash between the syllables. Circle the open syllable with the long *o* sound.

1. (ro)/bot
2. notify
3. polar
4. total
5. going
6. rodeo
7. Romeo
8. totem
9. over
10. moment
11. solo
12. poser
13. omen
14. Polish
15. global

C. Complete each sentence with a word from the box below. Then read the sentences out loud.

molar	moment	polar	robot	solar

1. A sudden bright spot on the sun is a _____solar_____ flare.

2. Plants and animals living near the north or south pole can be called

   _____.

3. If you can wait a _____ I will give you a ride.

4. A _____ is a tooth with a surface for grinding food.

5. Kate's mom has a _____ that vacuums their carpets.

D. Read the following words out loud. Circle the words with the /ō/ sound. Underline the word that have an open syllable with /ō/ spelled *o*.

(November)	local	toe	pole	grow	soap	moon	moan
sound	loud	load	toad	poem	group	soup	south
global	topaz	pony	torn	hotel	goat	crow	floats
phone	mow	go	how	hoe	vocal	opal	toast

Chapter 6 • Vowel Teams

Name _____ Date _____

WORD ANALYSIS: Open Syllables: Long *u*

A syllable ending with vowel sound is called an open syllable. When the open syllable has a long vowel sound, as in *unit*, it is usually stressed.

A. Read the following words out loud. Circle the open syllables.

cu/bic   tu/bu/lar   u/nit   hu/mid

B. Read the following words out loud. Put a slash between the syllables. Circle the open syllable with the long *u* sound.

1. (u)/ni/form   4. student   7. unity   10. futon   13. crucial

2. puny   5. dual   8. cruel   11. cubic   14. fuel

3. music   6. brutal   9. duplex   12. humid   15. human

C. Complete each sentence with a word from the box below. Then read the sentences out loud.

| Cupid   duel   human   music   pupil |

1. In Roman myths, _____*Cupid*_____ is a baby-faced god with a bow and arrow.

2. We spend some time each day listening to _____, just for the joy of it.

3. Light passes through the _____ located at the center of the iris.

4. The actors in the play had a _____ on stage.

5. To make a mistake just shows that you are _____.

D. Read the following words out loud. Circle the words with the /ū/ or /oo/ sound. Underline the words that have an open syllable with /ū/ spelled *u*.

(duty)   loose   lucid   cute   blue   grew   humane   Pluto

true   soup   tooth   tuna   hug   huge   crew   stupid

furnace   futile   cuckoo   mute   pool   tub   tube   due

duel   noodle   furnish   about   hunt   unit   Luke   drew

When two vowels appear together and have one sound, it is called a vowel team. Vowel teams can produce long vowel sounds, short vowel sounds, and other kinds of vowel sounds.

A. Read the following words out loud. Circle the words with the long vowel sound. Underline the words with the short vowel sound.

awful	donkey	head	suit
blue	enjoy	learn	they
book	fight	loud	thief
break	flood	meat	through
canoe	food	pie	toad
caught	gain	plaid	toe
cause	green	said	vein
choice	grew	say	weigh
crowd	grow	soup	wish

B. Write the words from Exercise A in the correct column in the chart below. After each word, write *L* for long, *S* for short, or *O* for other vowel.

a-sound	e-sound	i-sound	o-sound	u-sound	Other
break - L	donkey - L	fight - L	grow - L	blue - L	awful -O

C. Read the following words out loud. Draw lines to connect words that rhyme.

fruit   loan

shoe   toe

said   grew

grow   loot

grown   shed

WORD ANALYSIS: Cle Syllables

Usually when *-le* is at the end of a word, and it has a consonant before it, the consonant + *-le* form the last syllable. It usually has a schwa sound.

A. Read the following words with Cle syllables out loud. Circle the Cle syllable in each word.

-ble	-(c)kle	-dle	-fle	-gle	-ple	-s(t)le	-tle	-zle
able	tinkle	middle	waffle	giggle	simple	hassle	little	sizzle
bobble	pickle	huddle	ruffle	beagle	ample	whistle	title	muzzle
thimble	twinkle	paddle	rifle	angle	apple	measles	cattle	nozzle
bubble	ankle	meddle	stifle	tangle	ripple	tousle	bottle	puzzle

B. Read the following words out loud. Circle the Cle syllable in each. Then write a word that has the same Cle syllable.

1. sim(ple) **2.** tumble **3.** needle **4.** circle **5.** puzzle

crumple _____ _____ _____ _____

C. Complete each sentence with a word from the box below. Then read the sentences out loud.

| handles   little   riddle   rumble   stable   table |

1. A _____riddle_____ is a kind of short joke.

2. I'm not very hungry, so please give me a _____ piece of pie.

3. In the _____ you can grab a saddle for the horse.

4. I heard the _____ of thunder and saw a flash of lightning.

5. Use both _____ when you pick up that hot pot.

6. Let's gather around the _____ for supper at seven o'clock.

A. You will see these ten words in many books. Read the words out loud.

| aunt | beautiful | been | bread | brother | cousin | door | eyes | floor | house |

B. Read the words in the passage below. Underline the high frequency words.

Once upon a time, there was a house in the woods. In it lived a beautiful little girl named Opal, with hair and eyes so dark, they were almost black, and her brother, a woodsman named Ax. One day Ax sent Opal through the woods to their cousin and aunt's house with a basket of bread. When Opal had been knocking on her aunt's door for quite some time, she pushed the door open, and found her aunt in bed. "Oh, aunt, what big eyes you have." Opal said, looking at her aunt. "And what big teeth you have. And your hair looks like bear fur!" A big brown bear jumped to the floor and chased Opal around and around a chair. Ax, Auntie, and Cousin came home just in time to save Opal from the bear. Auntie and Cousin had been on their way to tell Ax about the bear just as Opal had been walking through the woods. They lived happily ever after, but only after they chased the bear out the back door and off into the woods.

C. Read the passage again. Answer the following questions.

1. Who lived in the house in woods?

   _____

2. Who saved Opal from the bear?

   _____

READING PRACTICE: Passage 13

A. Read the following passage out loud.

Plants and Our Lives

Although some plants are poison, many plants, and many more parts of plants, are edible. In fact, we could not live without plants, because everything we eat, except salt, comes from plants or eats plants to live. For example, chickens eat grains such as corn, and cattle eat grasses. You yourself eat many parts of many different plants day in and day out. You eat many kinds of roots, stems, leaves, flowers, and seeds.

Carrots and potatoes are common root vegetables. If you've eaten celery or asparagus, you've eaten a plant's stems. Lettuce is a leaf, and an apple is a fruit. Many fruits, such as apples, grapes, pears, and blueberries make tasty juices. Cauliflower is, well, as its name tells you, a flower. Peanut plants, the fruits of pumpkin vines, and sunflowers all contain edible seeds. Even mushrooms, although not classified as plants, depend on plants. When plants die, they become food for funguses such as mushrooms. All of this is part of the great cycle we call life.

B. Read the passage again. Answer the following questions.

1. What is this passage mostly about?

   _____

2. Why are plants important?

   _____

Home-School Connection Read the passage to a family member or a friend. Talk about your favorite fruits and vegetables. Do you both like the same ones?

A. Circle the correct word to complete each sentence. Then read the sentences out loud.

1. I got my brother a new (toi/**toy**) for his (**eighth**/aith) birthday.

2. It is a (rowbot/robot) (mowse/mouse).

3. It is made of (rubber/rubbur), so it can (bounce/bownce).

4. My brother took a (gud/good) (look/luck) at it.

5. He (chewed/chued) on his (fingernale/fingernail) and thought for a while.

6. Then he played (around/arowned) with the (controls/centrols) for a few minutes.

7. Suddenly, the toy hopped up and (doun/down) like a (kangaroo/kangaru).

8. My brother (shouted/showted) for everyone to come and (sea/see).

9. He made the mouse (goa/go) chasing after our (fear/feer) stricken cat.

10. The cat ran into the (closet/clauset) and hid among the (shues/shoes).

B. Correct the spelling of the underlined words. If the word is correct, put a check mark above it. Then read the paragraph out loud.

If you could <u>lern</u> something <u>noo</u>, what <u>wood</u> it be? You <u>cood</u> <u>larn</u> to <u>draw</u>. You <u>culd</u>
        1.   2.   3.   4. 5.   6.   7.

<u>lurn</u> to play a <u>moosical</u> instrument. You could even go on a <u>canoo</u> trip <u>doun</u> the river.
 8.   9.   10.   11.

Check <u>owt</u> your <u>local</u> <u>commyoonity</u> center. There's <u>allways</u> a class going on.
     12.   13.   14.   15.

CHAPTER 6 REVIEW (continued)

C. Read the following words out loud. Draw lines to connect words that rhyme.

1.	found	carol
2.	fee	eagle
3.	wonder	under
4.	nose	sea
5.	barrel	beak
6.	legal	steak
7.	wheel	noise
8.	toys	goes
9.	fake	shoe
10.	leek	steal
11.	blue	crowned

D. Read each clue. Unscramble the syllables and write the answer. Then read the answers out loud. Draw a slash to separate the syllables. Circle the open syllable.

1. a student	pilpu	_____ (pu)/pil _____
2. a notebook has this	perpa	_____
3. not a male	malefe	_____
4. no sound	lentsi	_____
5. Thanksgiving month	Nobervem	_____

CHAPTER 7 **SILENT LETTERS**

Silent *h*..154

Silent *l* 155

Silent *p* and *s*...156

Silent *t* 157

Silent *w* 158

Soft *c*...159

Soft *c* and Hard *c* 160

Soft *g*...161

Soft *g* (final *-ge* and *-dge*)......................................162

Soft *g* and Hard *g*..163

High Frequency Words: Set 14.................164

Reading Practice: Passage 14...................165

Final *-ve*..166

Blends with Three Letters (*str, spl, scr*) 167

Blends with Three Letters (*shr, thr*)............168

Chapter 7 Review...............................169

Name _____ Date _____

SILENT *h*

Sometimes the *h* is silent in words. The silent *h* often appears at the beginning of words.

A. Look at the pictures. Read the following words out loud. Then circle the letters that stand for the silent *h*.

herb

hour

B. Complete each sentence with a word from the box below. Then read the sentences out loud.

> herbivore   herbs   honest   honors   hours

1. If you tell the truth, you are _____.

2. An animal that eats only grass and leaves is a _____.

3. There are twenty-four _____ in a day.

4. Veteran's Day _____ those who served in the armed forces.

5. We grow _____ in our backyard.

C. Read the clues. Unscramble the answers in the right column. Write the word on the line. Then read the words out loud.

1. 24 in a day   urohs   _____

2. flavorful leaves   berhs   _____

3. truthful   nosthe   _____

4. animal that eats leaves   vorebiher   _____

5. highest respect   ronoh   _____

Name _____ Date _____

Sometimes the *l* is silent in words. The silent *l* often appears in the middle of words after a vowel.

A. Look at the pictures. Read the words that contain silent *l* out loud. Then circle the letters that stand for the silent *l*.

walk

salmon

B. Complete each sentence with a word from the box below. Then read the sentences out loud.

chalk   half   Stockholm   yolk

1. The yellow part of an egg is the _____.

2. Will you share _____ of your sandwich?

3. _____ is a city in Sweden.

4. Our teacher writes with _____ on the board.

C. Read the clues. Complete the puzzle with words from the box. Then read the words out loud.

almond   calm   chalk   stalk   walk

Across

3. type of nut
4. something that corn grows on

Down

1. not excited
2. you write on a blackboard with this
5. one foot in front of the other

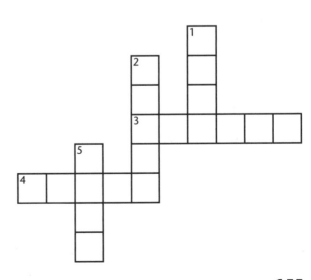

SILENT *p* and *s*

Sometimes the *p*, the *s*, or both the *p* and *s* are silent in words. The silent *p* and *s* can appear after a vowel or consonant.

A. Look at the pictures. Read the words out loud. Then circle the letters that stand for the silent *p*, silent *s*, or both.

raspberry

aisle

B. Complete each sentence with a word from the box below. Then read the sentences out loud.

cupboard   debris   Illinois   island   psalms   raspberries

1. Springfield is a city in the state of _____.

2. He jumped ship and swam to an _____.

3. In summer, _____ get ripe.

4. Please put these cans away in the _____ for me.

5. After the storm, the street was littered with _____.

6. The Greek meaning of _____ is "songs sung to a harp."

C. Read the clues. Unscramble the answers. Write the words on the lines. Then read the words out loud.

1. Little Rock is the capital   aaAknrss   _____

2. a red berry   yprasrrbe   _____

3. scattered bits of something broken   eibdrs   _____

4. shelf with doors   bpcuoadr   _____

5. armed forces unit   rposc   _____

SILENT *t*

Sometimes the *t* is silent in words. The silent *t* can appear at the beginning, in the middle, or at the end of words. It can appear after a vowel or a consonant.

A. Look at the pictures. Read the words out loud. Then circle the letters that stand for the silent *t*.

listen

ballet

B. Complete each sentence with a word from the box below. Then read the sentences out loud.

beret	buffet	crochet	debut	fasten	glistens	mortgage	soften

1. When making a cake, you need to _____ the butter.

2. My mom likes to _____ warm blankets from yarn.

3. At the party we served ourselves from the _____.

4. When you get into the car, you must _____ your seatbelt.

5. The sand at the beach always _____ on a sunny day.

6. A _____ is the very first night of a show or performance.

7. A new home loan is a _____ which a person pays back to a bank.

8. A _____ is a kind of French hat.

C. Read the clues. Unscramble the answers. Write the words on the lines. Then read the words out loud.

1. to make soft   tefson   _____

2. to hear   teslin   _____

3. food and drinks   teffub   _____

4. kind of dance   aetllb   _____

Chapter 7 • Silent Letters

SILENT w

Sometimes the *w* is silent in words. The silent *w* can appear at the beginning or in the middle of words.

A. Look at the pictures. Read the words out loud. Then circle the letters that stand for the silent *w*.

sword

writer

B. Complete each sentence with a word from the box below. Then read the sentences out loud.

| answer   two   who   whole   wrist   write   wrong |

1. I know the _____ to this question.

2. I will not get anything _____ on my test.

3. I must _____ neatly so my teacher can read my answers.

4. I only have _____ more questions to go.

5. Hooray! I completed the _____ test.

6. My _____ hurts from writing so much.

7. I want to know _____ got an A on the test.

C. Read the clues. Answer with words that contain the silent *w*. Then read the words out loud.

1. to respond

2. putting pen to paper

3. two halves

4. incorrect

5. contraction: *who + would*

			'	

Chapter 7   •   **Silent Letters**

SOFT c

The letter *c* can stand for the /s/ sound, as in *cement*. The letter *c* usually sounds like /s/ when it comes before *e, i,* or *y*. This sound is called the soft *c*.

A. Look at the pictures. Read the words out loud. Then circle the letters that stand for the soft *c*.

city

rice

cycle

B. Complete each sentence with a word from the box below. Then read the sentences out loud.

cells   ceramics   citizen   citrus   city   cycle   cyclone

1. Mom made this vase in her _____ class.

2. I live in the _____ of Cicero, Illinois.

3. I am a _____ of the United States of America.

4. Lemons and limes are _____ fruits.

5. _____ are the most basic units of life.

6. One _____ of our dryer was broken.

7. A _____ is a tropical storm with fast winds.

C. Read this grocery list out loud. Underline the words that contain the soft *c* sound.

Things to buy:		
two stalks of celery	citrus fruits	pecans
a bunch of carrots	cranberry juice	apple cider
a bag of crushed ice	allspice	four ripe juicy tomatoes
spicy Cajun shrimp	a piece of tuna	canned black beans
a whole chicken	sixteen ounces of walnuts	crisp iceberg lettuce

SOFT *c* and HARD *c*

The letter *c* stands for the /s/ sound when it comes before *e, i,* or *y,* as in *city.* This sound is called the soft *c.* The letter *c* stands for the /k/ sound when it comes before *a, o,* or *u,* as in *cut,* or before a consonant sound, as in *crisp.* This sound is called the hard *c.*

A. Look at the pictures. Read the words out loud. Then circle the letters that stand for the soft *c* sound and underline the letters that stand for the hard *c* sound.

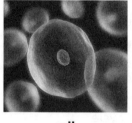
cell

lacy

cat

cot

B. Complete each sentence with a word from the box below. Then read the sentences out loud.

camped   can   celebrate   City   crunch

1. Tomorrow we will _____ my grandmother's 100th birthday.

2. After we returned from New York _____, we flew to Boston.

3. We _____ out in the woods last summer.

4. I hope you _____ come with us next time.

5. These crisp apples make a loud _____ when you bite into them.

C. Read the words in the box below out loud. Then write the words in the correct column.

call	cane	carpet	case
cause	cease	cell	cent
cite	city	cone	cost
count	crazy	crest	crust
curse	cute	cyberspace	fancy

Soft *c*	Hard *c*

Name _____ Date _____

SOFT *g*

The letter *g* can stand for the /j/ sound when it comes before *e, i,* or *y,* as in *germ.* This sound is called the soft *g.*

A. Look at the pictures. Read the words out loud. Then circle the letters that stand for the soft *g.*

gem

ginger

B. Complete each sentence with a word from the box below. Then read the sentences out loud.

> age   energy   gemstones   giant   gym   magic   stage

1. Yesterday we saw a _____ show.

2. Her necklace was made of _____ such as rubies and emeralds.

3. An elephant is a _____ next to a mouse.

4. We play basketball in our school's _____.

5. It is possible to generate _____ from wind and sunlight.

6. What _____ do you have to be to drive in your state?

7. The actors took the _____ for a final bow.

C. Underline the words that contain the soft *g,* as in *gem.* Then read the sentences out loud.

1. Today in gym class, Mr. Gentry decided to teach us to dance.

2. My partner was Gina. My legs were as wobbly as gelatin.

3. I held Gina's hand gently. Mr. Gentry asked us to be ladies and gentlemen.

4. Be an angel and hand this aged, fragile lady her reading glasses will you, dear?

5. General Gerald waged his war energetically.

SOFT *g* (final *-ge* and *-dge*)

The letters *-ge* and *-dge* stand for the /j/ sound. They appear at the end of a word, and the *e* is silent. Usually the vowel sound before *-ge* is long, as in *age*. The vowel sound before *-dge* is short, as in *budge*.

A. Look at the pictures. Read the words out loud. Then circle the letters that stand for the soft *g*.

huge

bridge

fudge

B. Complete each sentence with a word from the box below. Then read the sentences out loud.

badge   huge   judge   ridge   smudge   surgery   wedge

1. You can drive a _____*wedge*_____ into the log with the back of an ax.

2. You must show a _____ to go past the checkpoint at the airport.

3. Follow the trail along the high _____ and down into the valley.

4. The job of a _____ is to listen to evidence on both sides fairly.

5. She may need oral _____ on her wisdom teeth.

6. Tell him he has a _____ of grape jelly on his chin.

7. It would be a _____ mistake to skip class.

C. Read the clues out loud. Add *-ge* or *-dge* to complete the answers. Then read the words out loud.

1. This helps you cross to the other side.   bri_____

2. This means "very big."   hu_____

3. Your book has many of these.   pa_____

4. This person tells who is the best.   ju_____

5. This is a small house or cabin.   lo_____

Name _____ Date _____

SOFT *g* and HARD *g*

The letter *g* can stand for the /j/ sound when it comes before *e, i,* or *y,* as in *cage.* This sound is called the soft *g.* The letter *g* can stand for the /g/ sound when it comes before *a, o, u,* or before a consonant sound, as in *green.* This is called the hard *g.*

A. Look at the pictures. Read the words out loud. Then circle the letters that stand for the hard *g* and soft *g.*

gym

goat

glass

B. Complete each sentence with a word from the box below. Then read the sentences out loud.

| engaged   game   gave   gems   glad |

1. My dad _____ me a globe for my birthday.

2. I am _____ that we have no school today.

3. I enjoy a good _____ of chess.

4. My brother got _____ to his high school sweetheart.

5. I gave my mom earrings with small _____ in them.

C. List the words in the box below in the correct column on the chart. These words contain either the soft or hard *g* sound. Some words belong in both columns.

angel	age	agile	angle
budge	bugle	engage	geese
gel	gelatin	gentle	germ
get	gigantic	ginger	gland
goal	goat	grant	pager
rage	range	mug	sugar

Soft *g*	Hard *g*

A. You will see these ten words in many books. Read the words out loud.

against	cap	clothes	head	money
move	other	should	squirrel	water

B. Read the following passage out loud. Then circle the high frequency words.

Last year, at the state fair, I saw a trained squirrel ride a surfboard. The squirrel didn't have a lot of clothes, but he wore a little sailor's cap on his little gray head. I paid my money and went into a tent where there was a round swimming pool full of water. Other people gathered around the sides of the swimming pool with me. The squirrel-keeper started the motor on a little motorboat, and the boat started to move. The crowd in the back started to press against me when the squirrel hopped onto the water. I thought someone should tell them to move back because I was getting crushed. Soon, I forgot about the crowd. I thought the odds were against a squirrel learning to ride a surfboard. I honestly thought he would fail. But you should have seen that squirrel riding around and around without falling down. It was a real head-turner!

C. Read the passage again. Answer the following questions.

1. What was the squirrel wearing?

_____

2. What did the squirrel do that was so amazing?

_____

READING PRACTICE: Passage 14

A. Read the following passage out loud.

Jane Addams

Jane Addams, born in 1860, helped establish the concept of the community center in the United States. This is how it began.

In 1889, Addams rented a big house owned by Charles J. Hull in Cook County, Illinois. She thought that new Americans and other working class people needed a place to meet others, study, and enjoy the finer things in life. At the Hull House, Addams gave English classes to immigrants. People could also study dance, art, math, and music there. Immigrant residents at Hull House shared their cultures and languages with others. The Hull House became a center of culture for the city. Concerts were offered free to everyone, and clubs were started for children and adults.

In 1931, Addams received the Nobel Peace Prize for her work. Today, the Jane Addams Hull House still serves many people, although not in the same place it began.

B. Read the passage again. Answer the following questions.

1. What kinds of classes did Hull House provide?

   _____

2. Why did Addams start the community center?

   _____

Read the passage to a family member or a friend. Do you have a community center in your neighborhood? Discuss what events take place there.

FINAL -ve

Words with the pattern CVCe often have a long vowel sound, as in *gate, home,* and *drive.* When the letters *-ve* are at the end of a word, sometimes the vowel sound is short, as in *live.* When the letters *-ove* are at the end of a word, the *o* makes the short *u* sound, as in *glove.*

A. Look at the pictures. Read the words out loud. Then circle the short vowel sounds.

give

love

dove

B. Complete each sentence with a word from the box below. Then read the sentences out loud.

| above   covered   dove   gloves   have   hover   live |

1. The _____ is also a symbol for peace.

2. _____ will keep your hands warm when it is cold out.

3. I _____ in the small tan house on the corner.

4. I _____ a dog, a cat, and three fish as pets.

5. Let the rice simmer in a _____ pan on low heat.

6. On a clear night, you can see stars _____ your head.

7. The helicopter will _____ over the landing zone.

C. Some words that have -ve also have a long vowel sound. Some spellings have two pronunciations, and you must use the context to know which word is intended. Underline the words that <u>do not</u> have a long vowel sound. Circle words that have more than one pronunciation. Check your answers in a dictionary.

above	behave	cave	concave	cover	Dave	dive	diver	dove
gave	gavel	give	glove	grove	grovel	have	hive	hover
I've	live	liver	love	oven	over	pave	plover	river
save	seven	shove	solve	Steven	stove			

Name _____ Date _____

BLENDS with THREE LETTERS (*str, spl, scr*)

When a word begins with a consonant blend, two or three consonant sounds are blended together. Each consonant sound is pronounced.

- The letters *str* make the /s/ /t/ /r/ sound, as in *strong*.
- The letters *spl* make the /s/ /p/ /l/ sound, as in *splendid*.
- The letters *scr* make the /s/ /c/ /r/ sound, as in *scream*.

A. Look at the pictures. Read the words out loud. Then circle the blends.

strap

splash

scrub

B. Complete each sentence with a word from the box below. Write your own sentence using the words. Then read the sentences out loud.

scraps split string strong

1. Dad can _____*split*_____ a log in half with an ax.

   _____

2. My dad is so _____ he can lift his own weight over his head.

   _____

3. Small _____ of wood can help you get a fire started.

   _____

4. Dad ties the wood with thick _____.

   _____

C. Read the clues. Add *scr, spl,* or *str* to complete the answers.

1. to cut in two   _____it

2. not weak   _____ong

3. to rub clean   _____ub

4. where cars travel   _____eet

5. stir up water   _____ash

BLENDS with THREE LETTERS (*shr, thr*)

When a word begins with a consonant blend, two or three consonant sounds are blended together. When the digraphs *sh* or *th* are part of the consonant blend, the digraph makes a single sound.

- The letters *shr* make the /sh/ /r/ sound, as in *shrug*.
- The letters *thr* make the /th/ /r/ sound, as in *thrill*.

A. Look at the pictures. Read the words out loud. Then circle the blends.

shrimp

three

B. Complete each sentence with a word from the box below. Then write your own sentence using the word.

shrink   shrub   throat   throw

1. A _____*shrub*_____ is a woody plant or small bush.

_____

2. If you put that sweater in the dryer, it will _____.

_____

3. Don't _____ the ball too high.

_____

4. I have a cold, so my _____ hurts.

_____

C. Read the clues. Then write the word from the box that each clue describes.

shrink   shrimp   thread   thrill

1. a roller coaster ride   _____

2. a type of seafood   _____

3. use with a needle   _____

4. get smaller   _____

Chapter 7 • Silent Letters

CHAPTER 7 REVIEW

A. Complete each sentence with a word from the box below. Then read the sentences out loud.

ballet cob forced grocery ice island listen rice stage strange

1. What if you were stranded on a small _____?

2. There would be no _____ store.

3. You would not eat strawberry _____ cream.

4. You would not eat _____ and beans.

5. You would not eat corn on the _____.

6. You'd be _____ to eat coconuts all day.

7. You'd eat many _____ things, I suppose.

8. You could dance _____ if you wanted to.

9. You could sing and nobody would _____.

10. The whole island could be your _____.

B. Correct the spelling of the underlined words. If the word is correct, put a check mark over it. Then read the paragraph out loud.

Would you like to study in <u>Gurmany</u>? Many <u>exchang</u> programs offer you that <u>chans</u>. At
        1.   2.   3.

first you may not understand. Give it time. <u>Lisen</u> and observe how people speak. You will
                                   4.

soon speak the <u>languag</u>. You will feel <u>calm</u>. You will <u>anser</u> people when they speak to you.
          5.   6.   7.

C. Circle the correct word to complete each sentence. Then read the sentences out loud.

1. I have two pet (mis/mice).

2. Pinky and Charlie both have cute (fas/faces).

3. They live in a fancy (cage/caje) in my room.

4. I keep them in a warm (plas/place).

5. I have had them (since/sinc) May.

6. They like to (ras/race) on their wheels.

7. They hate white (ris/rice) but love cheese.

8. Their space is littered with (debris/debree).

9. I (change/chang) the bedding every week.

10. When their place is clean, they (danse/dance) and squeak.

D. Read the clues. Complete the puzzle with words from the box.

scrap shrinks splash squash strip three

Across

1. a bit of paper
4. number after two
5. to throw liquid

Down

1. a vegetable you eat in the fall
2. a comic _____
3. cotton _____ when you wash it

Chapter 7 • Silent Letters

CHAPTER 8 **WORD ANALYSIS**

Compound Words 172

Prefixes: *dis-, un-* 173

Prefixes: *over-, re-* 174

Prefix: *non-* 175

Suffixes: *-ness, -ful* 176

Suffixes: *-ly, -al* 177

Suffixes: *-ment, -ive* 178

Suffix: *-ion* 179

Suffixes: *-able, -ible* 180

Reading Practice: Passage 15 181

Reading Practice: Passage 16 182

Chapter 8 Review 183

COMPOUND WORDS

Compound words are made up of two or more words. There are three kinds of compound words:

- A solid compound is one word created from two words, as in *butterfly*.
- A hyphenated compound has a hyphen, as in *far-off*.
- An open compound has a space between the words but expresses one idea, as in *salad dressing*.

Solid	Hyphenated	Open
mail + box = **mailbox** lunch + box = **lunchbox** high + way = **highway**	close + up = **close-up** free + range = **free-range** one + way = **one-way**	African + American = **African American** voice + mail = **voice mail** whole + milk = **whole milk**

A. Read the following words out loud. Underline the compound words.

1. basket
2. rainbow
3. calculator
4. desktop

5. sunshine
6. wallpaper
7. cucumber
8. reading

9. firefighter
10. teacher
11. over there
12. over-the-top

13. underneath
14. under my desk
15. school day
16. newspaper

B. Read the following words out loud. Draw lines to connect the compound words. Then write the new word on the line.

1. back   pack   _____
2. air   line   _____
3. class   ground   _____
4. base   ball   _____
5. home   work   _____
6. play   room   _____

Chapter 8 • Word Analysis

PREFIXES: *dis-, un-*

The prefixes *dis-* and *un-* mean "the opposite of" or "not."

Base Word	*dis-*	*un-*
agree	disagree	—
happy	—	unhappy
baked	—	unbaked
appear	disappear	—
comfort	discomfort	—
lock	—	unlock

A. Complete each sentence by adding *dis-* or *un-* to the word in parentheses. Check for the correct spelling in a dictionary. Then read the sentences out loud.

1. (lock)   Will you help me _____ this door?

2. (infect)   We must _____ the cut on your arm.

3. (salted)   I eat _____ peanuts. I must not have salt.

4. (explored) In the wilderness, much of the land is _____.

5. (cooked)   Eating _____ eggs can make you sick.

6. (like)   I _____ the smell of garlic.

7. (wrap)   I will _____ my gifts now.

8. (true)   That story is false because it is simply _____.

B. Write your own sentence using each word. Then read your sentences out loud.

1. (unhappy)   _____

2. (disappear)   _____

3. (unable)   _____

4. (disrespect) _____

5. (unavailable) _____

Chapter 8 • Word Analysis

PREFIXES: *over-*, *re-*

The prefix *over-* means "too much" or "higher."

> **overeat** = to eat too much **overhead** = higher than your head

The prefix *re-* means "again."

> **reappear** = to appear again **revisit** = to visit again

A. Complete each sentence by adding *over-* or *re-* to the word in parentheses. Then read the sentences out loud.

1. (flow) The sink started to _____ and the rug got wet.

2. (seal) This bag has a zipper. I can _____ it.

3. (protect) My mom tends to _____ me.

4. (grown) The grass is _____ and needs to be cut.

5. (paint) After twenty years, it's time to _____ the house.

6. (glue) The title fell off my poster. I must _____ it.

B. Complete each sentence with a word from the box below. Then read the sentences out loud.

> overcook overdue overstay rephrase replay reprinted retake

1. The books must be returned to the library. They are _____.

2. I should leave now and not _____ my visit.

3. Please say that again. _____ it in simpler language.

4. Please don't _____ the rice.

5. I love that song. Will you _____ it for me?

6. The book was sold out. It had to be _____.

7. I failed the test. Tomorrow I will _____ it.

Name _____ Date _____

The prefix *non-* means "not." When *non-* is added to a base word, the new word means the opposite.

> **nonsense** = speech or writing that does not make sense
> **nonstick** = a coating that makes food not stick
> **nonsmoker** = someone who does not smoke

A. Complete each sentence by adding *non-* to the word in parentheses. Write your own sentence using the new word. Then read the sentences out loud.

1. (profit) Our club raises money to give it away. We are a _____ club.

_____

2. (stop) It was a _____ flight from New York to Madrid.

_____

3. (fat) _____ milk, or skim milk, does not contain any fat.

_____

4. (verbal) When you use body language, you talk in a _____ way.

_____

B. Read the clues. Add the prefix *non-* to the words in the box. Complete the puzzle with the new words.

> ____criminal   ____living
> ____toxic   ____dairy
> ____fat

Across

3. not a criminal

5. no fat

Down

1. not alive

2. no milk or cheese

4. not poison

SUFFIXES: -ness, -ful

The suffix *-ness* means "the condition of being." It is added to an adjective to make a noun. For example, *sadness* means "the condition of being sad." If the base word ends in a consonant and *y*, change the *y* to *i* before adding *-ness*.

> happy + *-ness* = **happiness**   silly + *-ness* = **silliness**

The suffix *-ful* means "full of." It is added to a noun to make an adjective. For example, *joyful* means "full of joy." If the base word ends in a consonant and *y*, change the *y* to *i* before adding *-ful*.

> plenty + ful = **plentiful**   beauty + ful = **beautiful**

A. Complete each sentence by adding *-ness* or *-ful* to the word in parentheses. Then read the sentences out loud.

1. (flavor)   The peach was delicious and very _____.

2. (weak)   The student didn't do well in math. It was his _____.

3. (empty)   The room had no furniture. The _____ made the room look big.

4. (good)   Taste the _____ of homemade cookies.

5. (plenty)   Apples are _____ in the fall.

B. Write your own sentences with words from the box below. Then read the sentences out loud.

| beautiful | bountiful | colorful | forgetful | goodness |
| greediness | happiness | mournful | thoughtful | weakness |

1. _____

2. _____

3. _____

4. _____

5. _____

Chapter 8 • Word Analysis

SUFFIXES: -ly, -al

The suffix *-ly* means "in a certain way." It is used to form an adverb. For example, *sadly* means "in a sad way." If the base word ends in a consonant and *y*, change the *y* to *i* before adding *-ly*.

```
happy + -ly = happily      angry + -ly = angrily
```

The suffix *-al* means "like or of." For example, *musical* means "of music." Sometimes the base word needs a spelling change. If the base word ends in an *e*, drop the *e* before adding *-al*. If the base word ends in a consonant and *y*, change the *y* to *i* before adding *-al*.

```
arrive + -al = arrival      deny + -al = denial
```

A. Complete each sentence by adding *-ly* or *-al* to the word in parentheses. Write your own sentence using the new word. Then read the sentences out loud.

1. (nature)   This fruit bar is made with all _____ flavors.

_____

2. (arrive)   When Mom returned, we were all there for her _____.

_____

3. (hungry)   The stray dog _____ chewed on the bone.

_____

4. (logic)   Your ideas are not _____.

_____

B. Read the clues. Unscramble the letters. The answers contain the suffix *-ly* or *-al*. Write each answer on the line.

1. not quickly   lolswy   _____

2. having to do with industries   ridusintal   _____

3. the least possible   alnimim   _____

4. in a gentle way   lygent   _____

5. having magic   icamalg   _____

SUFFIXES: *-ment, -ive*

The suffix *-ment* means "the condition of being." It is added to a verb to make a noun. For example, *disappointment* means "the condition of being disappointed." If the base word ends in an *e*, drop the *e* before adding *-ment*.

argue + *-ment* = **argument**   enjoy + *-ment* = **enjoyment**

The suffix *-ive* means "having to do with." It is added to a verb to make an adjective. For example, *instinctive* means "having to do with instinct." If the base word ends in *e*, drop the *e* before adding *-ive*.

relate + *-ive* = **relative**   coerce + *-ive* = **coercive**

A. Complete each sentence by adding *-ment* or *-ive* to the word in parentheses. Then read the sentences out loud.

1. (amuse)   We went to an _____ park on Sunday.

2. (act)   Now that the baby is walking, she's very _____.

3. (disrupt) The student was _____ in class.

4. (amaze) I watched in _____ as the dog played gently with the cat.

B. Read the clues. Add the suffix *-ment* or *-ive* to the words in the box. Make necessary spelling changes. Complete the puzzle with the new words.

construct_____	employ_____
negate_____	ship_____
expense_____	

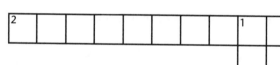

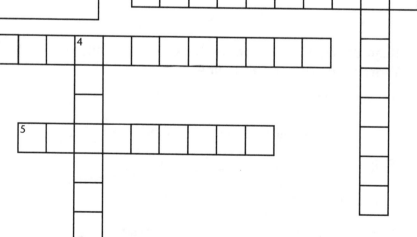

Across

2. a job
3. useful
5. costs a lot

Down

1. not positive
4. something that is shipped

WORD ANALYSIS: Suffix *-ion*

The suffix *-ion* shows an action, result, or state. It is added to a verb to make a noun. When the base word ends in an *e*, drop the *e* before adding *-ion*.

Base Word	*-ion*
pollute	pollution
perfect	perfection
possess	possession
impress	impression
confuse	confusion

A. Complete each sentence by adding *-ion* to the word in parentheses. Write your own sentence using the new word. Then read the sentences out loud.

1. (profess) Teaching is a noble _____.

   _____

2. (adopt) The _____ process will take two years.

   _____

3. (discuss) We had a long _____ about math grades.

   _____

4. (imitate) I can do a good _____ of the teacher.

   _____

5. (instruct) Please find the _____ manual and read it to me.

   _____

B. Correct the spelling of the underlined words. If the word is correct, put a check mark over it. Then read the paragraph out loud.

You have good news, don't you? I can tell by the <u>expretion</u> on your face. What? You got
  _{1.}

a <u>promosion</u>? <u>Congratulations</u>! What? We're moving to a new <u>location</u>? Well, let's have a
  _{2.}   _{3.}   _{4.}

<u>discution</u> about it first.
  _{5.}

SUFFIXES: -able, -ible

The suffixes -able and -ible mean "can be done." They are added to verbs to make adjectives. The suffixes sound the same, so they can be difficult to spell. Most of the time, if the root is a complete word, add -able. If the root is not a complete word, add -ible. There are more words with -able than -ible.

Root	-able	-ible
understand	understandable	—
comfort	comfortable	—
enjoy	enjoyable	—
vis-	—	visible
terr-	—	terrible
poss-	—	possible

A. Circle the correct word to complete each sentence. Write your own sentence using the word. Then read the sentences out loud.

1. I have a pen that uses (invisible/invisable) ink.

   _____

2. My dad purchased a small, (affordible/affordable) car.

   _____

3. The sunset on the beach was (incredable/incredible).

   _____

4. The dress is (washible/washable) in cold water.

   _____

5. Our car is old, but at least it's (dependible/dependable).

   _____

B. Add -able or -ible to complete each word. Then read the paragraph out loud.

It's imposs_____ to go anywhere with my little brother. He can't be near anything
   1.

break_____. It's not that he's irrespons_____. He's only four years old. Mom says
   2.   3.

his behavior is understand_____. But when I break something, I wish I were
   4.

invis_____.
   5.

READING PRACTICE: Passage 15

A. Read the following passage out loud.

A New Friend

Ray was bored, bored, bored. In the middle of winter vacation, both of his buddies were out of town. Jake was visiting his grandmother. Tom was in Alaska. Ray stared out the window at the new snow. Right now, they would all be snowboarding or having a snowball fight.

Ray went outside. Everything was quiet after the snowfall. He walked up the block, past Jake's house, past Tom's house. Then he saw someone ahead, rolling a ball of snow in a yard. It was a boy about his age.

The boy smiled and said, "Hey, I'm Steve. I'm visiting from Oregon. This snow is awesome. Do you want to help me make a fort?" Ray decided that today would be a perfect day to make a fort with a new friend.

B. Read the passage again. Answer the following questions.

1. Why is Ray bored?

   _____

2. What does Ray decide to do after he meets Steve?

   _____

Home-School Connection Read the passage to a family member or a friend. Talk about a time you made a new friend.

A. Read the following passage out loud.

The Black Widow

Most people try to avoid spiders, and one of the most disliked is the black widow spider. A black widow has a glossy black body with a red hourglass shape on its belly. Think of this red shape as a warning sign: Stay away! A bite from a female black widow spider contains poison, and it is painful. This bite can make you very sick, but it is unlikely to kill you, because the amount of venom is fairly small.

The black widow spider makes cobwebs rather than spiderwebs. That means the webs of the black widow do not follow any pattern. They lack both shape and form.

The female black widow spider has a reputation for not being a very friendly mate. Just think about its name. But, in fact, there are three species of black widow spiders in the United States, and in only one of these species does the female kill the male after mating.

B. Read the passage again. Answer the following questions.

1. How does the black widow spider get its name?

   _____

2. Why is this spider dangerous to humans?

   _____

Read the passage to a family member or a friend. Has that person ever seen a black widow spider? Have you? What other poisonous animals do you know of?

Name _____ Date _____

A. Complete each sentence by adding *dis-, un-, re-,* **or** *over-* **to the word in parentheses. Then read the sentences out loud.**

1. Mom was (happy) _____ with the score on my math test.

2. She wants me to (take) _____ the test.

3. I don't want Mom to (react) _____.

4. On the other hand, I don't want to (obey) _____ her.

5. My teacher was (joyed) _____ that I wanted a better grade.

6. "Look at your test again," she said. "(view) _____ it."

7. I saw that I had (looked) _____ the other side!

8. "You didn't finish. Your test is (finished) _____," said my teacher.

9. "Sit down. Do the other side. Make your bad grade (appear) _____."

10. Wow! A second chance! This is (expected) _____!

B. Correct the spelling of the underlined words. If the word is correct, put a check mark over it. Then read the paragraph out loud.

Homeschooling is the <u>educasion</u> of children at home. Homeschooling is an <u>opsion</u>
                1.   2.

for parents who need a <u>flexable</u> schedule. Homeschooling may also involve <u>instruction</u> at
                3.   4.

home under the <u>supervition</u> of a formal school. Often, homeschooling parents get together
              5.

and have <u>discussions</u>. They pool their <u>valuible</u> resources to provide the best for their
      6.   7.

children.

C. Circle the correct word to complete each sentence. Then read the sentences out loud.

1. At my house, everyone is (responsable/responsible) for the chores.

2. When paint is chipping, Dad (repaints/nonpaints).

3. Lynn uses a (nonstick/unstick) pan to make breakfast.

4. We have a garden, so vegetables are (plentyful/plentiful).

5. My favorite are the (colorful/colorfull) bell peppers.

6. Our apples signal the (arriveal/arrival) of fall.

7. We harvest the fruits and vegetables (quickly/quickful).

8. We conserve the (freshness/freshfull) by drying the fruit.

9. These types of snacks are delicious and (inexpensive/inexpenseful).

10. We had a most (enjoyible/enjoyable) time.

D. Read the clues out loud. Unscramble the syllables to find the answer. Write each word on the line. Underline each suffix. Then read the words out loud.

1. lack of strength   wnesseak   _____

2. a party   letioncebra   _____

3. pretty   aufulbeti   _____

4. a job   mentployem   _____

5. in a hungry way   lygrihun   _____

CONSONANT REMINDERS

Consonant Sound-Spellings

/b/ b	**b**ird
/d/ d	**d**ollar
/f/ f, ph	**f**arm, **ph**one
/g/ g	**g**olf
/h/ h	**h**ead
/j/ j, g, ge, dge	**j**oke, **g**erm, hu**ge**, bri**dge**
/k/ c, ck, k	**c**omputer, ro**ck**et, **k**itten
/l/ l	**l**emon
/m/ m	**m**ath
/n/ n, kn, gn	**n**urse, **kn**ees, si**gn**
/p/ p	**p**encil
/r/ r, wr	**r**ight, **wr**ong
/s/ s, c	**s**andwich, **c**enter
/t/ t	**t**ime
/v/ v	**v**isit
/w/ w	**w**orld
/y/ y	**y**oung
/z/ z, s	**z**one, girl**s**

Consonant Digraphs

/ch/ ch, tch	**ch**ildren, wi**tch**
/sh/ sh	**sh**oe
/th/, /ᵵh/ th	**th**ank (voiceless), **th**ey (voiced)
/hw/ wh	**wh**y
/ng/ ng, n	hu**ng**er, bli**n**k

Consonant Generalizations

When two of the same consonants appear together in a word, only one is heard, as in *drummer*.

When the letter *c* is followed by the vowels *a* or *o*, the *c* stands for the /k/ sound, as in **c**at and **c**otton.

When the letter *c* is followed by the vowels *e* or *i*, the *c* stands for the /s/ sound, as in **c**ent and **c**ity.

When the letters *c* and *h* appear next to each other in a word, they stand for the /ch/ sound, as in **ch**icken.

When the letter *g* is followed by the vowels *e* or *i*, the *g* usually stands for the /j/ sound, as in **g**entle and **g**iant.

VOWEL REMINDERS

Short Vowel Sound-Spellings

/a/ a   chat
/e/ e   neck
/i/ i   list
/o/ o   clock
/u/ u   luck

Long Vowel Sound-Spellings

/ā/ a, a_e, ay, ai   acorn, brave, stay, wait
/ē/ e, ee, ea, ie, ey, y   she, agree, jeans, puppies, monkey, silly
/ī/ i, i_e, igh, ie, y   wild, dime, light, tries, why
/ō/ o, o_e, oa, ow, oe   cold, note, throat, known, toe
/ū/ u, u_e, oo, ew, ui, oe   human, cute, moon, few, fruit, shoe

Vowel Team Sound-Spellings

/ou/ ou, ow   house, crowded
/aw/ aw, au   lawn, cause
/oi/ oi, oy   coin, enjoy
/oo/ oo   foot

R-Controlled Vowel Sound-Spellings

/är/ ar   party
/ôr/ or, ore, our   sports, more, four
/ûr/ er, ir, ur, ear, or, ar   serve, birthday, Thursday, learn, work, calendar
/âr/ air, are   chair, square

VOWEL GENERALIZATIONS

If there is one vowel in a stressed syllable, the vowel usually has a short sound, as in *little*.

When a word has only one vowel, the vowel sound is usually short, as in *cub*.

When a word has a double *e* (*ee*), these letters stand for the long *e* sound, as in *meet*.

When two vowels appear together in a word, the first vowel is usually a long sound and the second vowel is usually silent, as in *please*.

Syllable Reminders

There are six types of syllables:

Closed: CVC, CCVC, CVCC, CCVCC	cat, stop, milk, spend
Open: CV, CCV	**pi**lot, **stu**dent
Vowel-Silent *e*: CVCe, CCVCe, CVCCe	sale, broke, paste
Vowel Team: CVVC, CCVVC, CVVCC	team, proof, fault
R-Controlled: CVrC, CCVrC, CVrCC	sort, smart, torch
Consonant-*le* : Cle, CCle	**puzzle**, ge**ntle**

SYLLABLE GENERALIZATIONS

In a word with two or more syllables, one syllable receives more stress than the other or others.

Inflectional endings such as *-ed, -ing, -es,* prefixes, and suffixes often form separate syllables.

If the first vowel sound in a word is followed by two consonants, the first syllable usually ends with the first of the two consonants, as in *rib/bon*.

If the first vowel sound in a word is followed by a single consonant, that consonant usually begins the second syllable, as in *pa/per*.

In most two-syllable nouns, the first syllable is stressed, as in *pencil, doghouse, female*.

When the last syllable is the /r/ sound, the syllable is usually unstressed, as in *sister*.

When a two-syllable word ends with a consonant and a *y*, the first syllable is usually stressed and the last syllable is usually unstressed, as in *puppy*.